SKY DIVING IN 8 DAYS

Miles Clark

SKY DIVING

IN 8 DAYS

OSPREY

For Sarah

who regarded jumping out of planes as rather strange, but kindly agreed to marry me anyway

Published in 1989 by Osprey Publishing Limited
59 Grosvenor Street
London W1X 9DA

British Library in Publication Data

Clark, Miles
Sky diving in 8 days.
1. Free-fall parachuting
I. Title
797.5'6

ISBN 0-540-07426-8

Filmset by Tameside Filmsetting Limited
Printed in Great Britain by BAS Printers Limited,
Over Wallop, Hampshire, Great Britain

Front cover: Jake Rickwood
Illustrations: Alan Burton

Photography by Simon Ward

CONTENTS

INTRODUCTION

From high overhead came a series of short, heavy fluttering sounds and three rectangular parachutes – two red and one blue – simply erupted out of thin air. Suspended from each was a tiny black dot, and for three minutes or so, they swayed and zig-zagged across the sky, growing steadily larger. Eventually, each dot expanded into a crooked human figure, until finally, one by one, they came sailing in over the trees to touch down in the field beyond the stream.

Even in the imagination, the idea of descending gently out of a cloudless blue sky, with the world spread out below your feet, has a dream-like appeal. I had always assumed that this was what made parachutists go parachuting. And yet, for a seasoned skydiver, that moment – half a mile above the earth – when the parachute blooms above his head, is not the beginning of the jump, but the end. The most exhilarating moments are the precious seconds in freefall before the canopy has to be deployed; and ironically, for most parachutists, a parachute is simply the safest and easiest way to get back to the ground.

Recently, the skills of manoeuvring a parachute – both for accuracy, and in linking parachutes in the sky – have become more and more popular. But it's still the thought of falling out of the sky, of plummeting to earth at over twice the motorway speed limit, that fires the public imagination.

Not long ago there was still only one way that people could be introduced to parachuting – a well proven but lengthy version of the basic military training method. Over the last 20 years, millions have completed the first stage of this course and found themselves beside the cold doorway of a light plane, 2,000 ft above the ground. All of them felt hollow and weak as they launched themselves into the white silence; and all of them have felt the massive relief when two and a half seconds later, their parachute was opened automatically by a 'static line' fixed to the aircraft's fuselage. For many of them, that first jump, with just 2½ seconds in freefall, will be their only contact with the sport.

But for committed beginners, the aim has always been to progress through a series of stages or 'categories', to longer periods and more advanced manoeuvres in freefall. The final goal is to emerge as a fully-qualified skydiver.

It's rare for anyone to earn that qualification in less than 35 jumps. A faultless student might do it in perhaps 25; others have taken as many as 90; and that can take up to a year.

A Static Line student, on the more conventional introduction to skydiving, yells his way into the deep blue yonder. A line fixed to the aircraft's fuselage is deploying his main parachute automatically after just 2½ seconds in freefall.

There is still no gentle approach to parachuting; but eight years ago a very different alternative developed in America – a course in which not just one, but two instructors will hold your hand and say nice things to you as you jump.

To the amazement of even some of the most experienced skydivers, the *Accelerated Freefall Course (AFF)* suddenly enabled the first time jumper – firmly held throughout the dive by two highly-experienced instructors – to freefall from 12,000 ft, within a few hours of walking onto a drop zone.

Accelerated Freefall (AFF) is a rapid progression course, hence its rather unnerving name – the learning process, rather than the dive, is accelerated. In contrast to the conventional Static Line course, AFF condenses the training into a few hours of intensive one-to-one coaching. Given good weather, a faultless student could conceivably achieve that Category 8 in as few as *seven* jumps and seven days; the average is between ten and 12 jumps over a week to ten days.

The course is divided into seven grades or levels, culminating in an eighth qualifying dive. All the jumps are carried out from above 9,000 ft, which, in the words of one AFF brochure, 'allows maximum freefall time in which to relax and practise the exercises that you've been taught.'

If you're impatient about getting on to freefall, or simply have very little spare time, AFF is the perfect answer. And were it not for the cost for the ten to 12 jumps that it normally takes to qualify – everyone would be doing it.

Since 1986, there has been one other option: *Tandem Jumping* is aimed at the sort of person who may not have the time, the interest or the money to complete a full course, but who wants, just once, to experience the exhilaration of freefall. The training – it's more of a briefing – takes just 20 minutes. Using a special dual harness, the student is linked to the front of a qualified instructor or 'Tandem Master'. From the time they leave the aircraft, throughout the freefall (which may last as long as a minute) and a gentle, controlled landing under a single specially-designed canopy, the Tandem Master is entirely responsible for all aspects of the dive.

Friends have said, 'You're so brave. I could *never* do that.' I'm certainly not and they certainly could. Almost everyone who has picked up this book is potentially a skydiver. If the truth be known, making the effort to telephone a parachute centre for some details is probably the bravest thing you'll do. Fitness, physique, age, health and temperament make very

Flying united: a Tandem Jump is the quickest way to experience the thrill of freefall. The tape above this Tandem Master's back leads to a small drogue 'chute which reduces their rate of fall to that of a single skydiver.

few exclusions. There are medical exclusions but blind and physically-handicapped students have already made AFF jumps. Skydiving or Sport Parachuting – there's no distinction – has had a difficult childhood. For 25 years, the pastime in which people 'throw themselves out of a perfectly serviceable aircraft' has had to suffer a dare-devil and death-defying image.

As a rule, skydivers don't spare much time for the statistics of their sport; and with some justification: the chances of 'bouncing' are now extremely slim – typically, if it means anything to you, one fatality in 90,000 jumps.

In the last five years, the technological evolution in the sport has been very rapid; and according to Jack Gregory, one of the American pioneers of AFF, the over-riding factor in injuries and fatalities in the sport is human error.

'The equipment has reached a point where, properly maintained and properly used, there's only the smallest chance of having a problem. Nothing is perfect in life,' he says. 'Parachutes or politics, things will go wrong; and I never tell people that parachuting is 100 per cent safe, because I'd be lying. I've seen people die doing it. But it's as safe as you can make it.'

A handful of people are killed in parachuting accidents every year. Each victim, duly – and quite correctly – makes a posthumous appearance in the papers. But often it's not the fact that they appear, but the *way* that they appear in the press – as though each was innocently and unwittingly sent to their deaths – that provides the armchair critics with the 'facts and figures'.

According to Jack Gregory, the figures prove one point: that much the most dangerous thing that skydivers do is drive to and from the airfield. Parachuting isn't rash or irresponsible – and suggesting that all skydivers are hotheads and danger-lovers would be as like branding all sports fans as hooligans.

My introduction to AFF came at a little aerodrome in England called Headcorn. These few acres of Kent countryside and the 13,000 ft column of air above them, are occupied for 12 months of the year by a dedicated group of several hundred skydivers; and it was on this drop zone, in February 1985, that Accelerated Freefall was introduced to Britain.

Now, three years later, the Slipstream Adventures School of Accelerated Freefall at Headcorn is the largest AFF school in the United Kingdom, training around 60 students a year. In nearly 17,000 descents made at the club in 1986, there were just 13 injuries, only one involving a broken limb. In 1989, there was a freak fatal accident. But not one injury at Headcorn in five years and over 100,000 descents has been entirely the fault of equipment failure. It was here that I learnt to freefall in eight days.

Miles Clark with the instructors of the Headcorn Parachute Club and Slipstream Adventures, the most active AFF centre in Britain.

- ☐ Plenty of fresh country air
- ☐ Crossing the Whuffo line
- ☐ Straight into harness
- ☐ Preparing for Level 1
- ☐ Canopies and cutaway drills
- ☐ Sensory overload
- ☐ 'A meticulously checked assumption'

DAY ONE

If all goes well, six hours or so into an Accelerated Freefall Course, you will find yourself facing the open door of a small plane, 12,000 ft above the ground. To left and right of you, grinning confidently, are two of the most highly-qualified skydivers in the world.

In front of you, framed in the doorway, is a vast, cold emptiness; the ground, now two and a half miles below, is far too distant to lend familiarity to the scene. At this point, most first-time jumpers are staring huge-eyed into the wilderness of the clouds, wearing the vacant expression of the man who has just realised he's on the wrong train. One of the instructors will peer out over the sill of the door, watching the ground until the aircraft is exactly the right distance upwind of the drop zone. When the instant arrives, he'll press a small button on the wall of the fuselage. The engine noise will fall away, flooded out by the blustering of the slipstream. One instructor will nod to the other; they'll take a firm grip of the handles on your legs and all three of you prepare to fall away from the aircraft together. Finally, a smiling goggled face will come to within six inches of yours, and shout the devastating question,

'*Are you ready to skydive?*'

In a hollow voice that you won't recognise, you'll hear yourself accept the invitation.

'*Then put your legs out after me!*'

Your legs slide out into the 70 mile an hour blast of

the slipstream. And in those four seconds, you are irreversibly committed to the most extraordinary experience of your life.

It was very strange. From the moment I knew I'd be doing an Accelerated Freefall course, it had never occurred to me that it would be anything other than massively safe. It was the reactions of friends and relations that began to make me wonder. For at least a week before the course, people who'd never before shown me any special affection or concern for my health, began to shake me slowly by the hand or, glassy-eyed, plant kisses on both cheeks. These were accompanied by softly-spoken remarks like, 'Goodbye – we'll see you again sooner or later', until it reached the stage where I felt a bit like a Kamikaze pilot coming to the end of summer leave. In the end, it was easier just to tell them that I was going away to get plenty of fresh country air.

As it turned out, the Monday morning was miserable. I arrived at Headcorn half an hour early; and since there was still only a few people about, I wandered around the airfield.

It had just stopped raining and the air was heavy with the smell of grass. Beside the large grey dome of a hangar, dozens of light aircraft were sitting obediently in ranks along the edge of the airstrip, gently dripping. There was a bright red fire-engine, with *Headcorn Aerodrome Fire Service* painted in gold letters down its side. Three portable homes sat side by side, white and characterless like giant sugar lumps.

Nearby was a curious collection of buildings, two rows of red-brick huts facing each other across a cracked concrete alleyway, punctuated here and there by clumps of grass. The roof of a third hut had sprouted a cluster of metal stalks, crowned with antennae and anenometers.

To anyone who hadn't read the signs above the doors, this could easily have been a hutted transit camp for troops; or a twin row of disused stables. Once, in fact, these were hopper huts, temporary accommodation for families from London's East End, who came down to pick hops in September. To the instructors and pilots who live in the rooms on either side of it now, the red-brick alleyway is known simply as Skid Row. Two small offices – each the size of a potting shed – face each other at one end. Since 1983, they have been the home of the Headcorn Parachute Club and the Slipstream Adventures School of Accelerated Freefall. One thing puzzled me; a small black notice, nailed to the fence around a large paved area. In bold white lettering were the words:

*No Dogs, No Kids and No Whuffos
Beyond This Point*

I was still trying to work it out when someone spoke behind me; a short man in a red jump suit who wasn't wasting much time in starting my education.

'That sign marks the Whuffo Line,' he said folding his arms. 'You see, the world is divided into two sorts of people – Skydivers and Whuffos.'

From his tone, he clearly felt that between the two of us, mankind was well represented. A Whuffo, I was told, is anyone who doesn't jump out of planes. It comes from the question so often asked of American skydivers:

'What for [whuffo] you jump out of planes, Mister?'

And needless to say, if you have to ask what it means. . .

A Whuffo I certainly was – my ignorance was total. I'd never even seen a parachute, much less entrusted my life to one. What, for instance, does a skydiver wear when he's skydiving? Or even when he isn't? How cold is it, when you're plummeting towards the countryside? How many seconds do you plummet for? And when – or even how – do you decide that it would be better for your health if you stopped plummeting and started dangling instead? Then there were the less earth-shattering questions: could I wear spectacles when falling to earth at 120 mph? Did skydiving invalidate a life assurance policy?

Fortunately, I wasn't alone in my ignorance. I was joined on the course by Stephen Saberi, a 22 year-old chemistry research student, who'd decided that even if it meant living on baked beans for a year, he'd find the money to put himself through the AFF course.

In the last three months, Steve had made a dozen or so static line jumps; but like so many students on the conventional course, he'd reached a certain stage in the training and got stuck. For jump after jump, he was unable to prove to the instructors that he was ready to progress to the next stage or 'category'. And although he was determined that sooner or later, he'd get on to unsupervised freefall, twelve weeks on the static line course was all he'd been able to stand.

'I'm just impatient,' he admitted. 'Basically, I like to run before I can walk, and I just got fed up with the length of time it was taking.'

When he'd first heard about AFF though, there had been plenty of doubts: 'Quite apart from the cost, I felt that if I couldn't even get it right by learning through the slow conventional method, what was the point of trying an Accelerated Freefall Course?'

In the end, someone had persuaded him that AFF's intensive personalised coaching was just what he needed: on the ground, he would have his own 'coach'; and in the air he'd be held in the correct position by two instructors and guided throughout the dive.

At the same time, we'd both discovered that Slipstream Adventures in Kent – part-owned by Headcorn Parachute Club, and operating with the same aircraft – is the largest School of Accelerated Freefall and Tandem in Britain. Of the six instructors who work for the company on a regular basis – with more than 16,000 descents between them – some are on the full-time staff of the Headcorn Parachute Club, and others, like Jane Buckle, are freelance.

Jane was to be my instructor for the week; and although, at 29, she has been four times British Ladies Skydiving Champion, with more than 3,000 descents in her logbook, that in itself would not be enough to qualify her as an AFF Instructor.

'The AFF Instructor rating,' she says, 'is much the most difficult that I've had to get. For starters, you need a minimum of 1,000 jumps and *ten hours* in freefall. And then there's the course itself. Most of the instructors at Headcorn have over 2,000 jumps behind them. So you're not in the hands of amateurs.'

The nerve centre of Slipstream Adventures is a low-ceilinged ten-by-ten room at the end of Skid Row. Around the white-washed walls are clip-framed photographs, of human insects, with faces distorted into wind-creased smiles, frozen in flight, somewhere among the clouds. Sometimes there were two people, flying united, hooked together for the descent. But always, the background was slightly different. Here, an impossible human jigsaw puzzle had been linked together a mile above an archipelago of tropical islands. And there, a formation of 20 or 30 bodies in pick-and-mix colours was framed by the triangular grey scars of runway tarmac.

We filled in forms, a green one, an orange one and a white one, all promising slightly different things or accepting various conditions.

For the whole of that first morning, Jane took us through our initial ground training; the equipment, aircraft emergency drills, canopy deployment, canopy control, obstacle avoidance, safety checks and landing. She began with a warning:

'I'm afraid that parachuting in the UK is very

weather-dependent. It doesn't actually affect the training at all, but it does affect the jumping. You'll find out very quickly that parachutists are optimists; we always anticipate that the weather's going to get better. Obviously, much of the time it doesn't, but we'll always stay here until it's dark.'

She produced a neat red harness complete with parachute container and placed it at our feet.

'Now, the kit that we give you is exactly the same as an experienced jumper would wear, but with some added safety features which I'll explain to you. Every experienced jumper you see walking around here will be wearing a rig which looks just like this.'

It was impossibly small. More like a rucksack that someone had forgotten to pack than a state-of-the-art freefall rig. Technology had been trimming and tightening until the optimum design had been reached.

'It's called a Chaser,' she said, 'and you'll find that most people on this drop zone jump either this type of parachute or another version of it – the Racer or the Tracer; they're exactly the same rig, just made by other companies. You can always recognise them; they've got this round circle at the top which is the pilot chute of the reserve parachute. It's called the Pop Top; 90 per cent of the instructors jump this type of rig as well. Normally you wouldn't jump this sort of rig until you've qualified; but in AFF, you go

Opposite Six essentials for human flight: a rig (main and reserve parachutes) from £1,200; an altimeter (from £50), a hard helmet (from £25), goggles (from £5), gloves (from £15) and jumpsuit (from £85). An AFF centre will provide you with all of them until you have qualified.

Below The reserve canopy is contained in the upper part of the rig. The circular pad, or Pop Top, is the reserve canopy pilot chute.

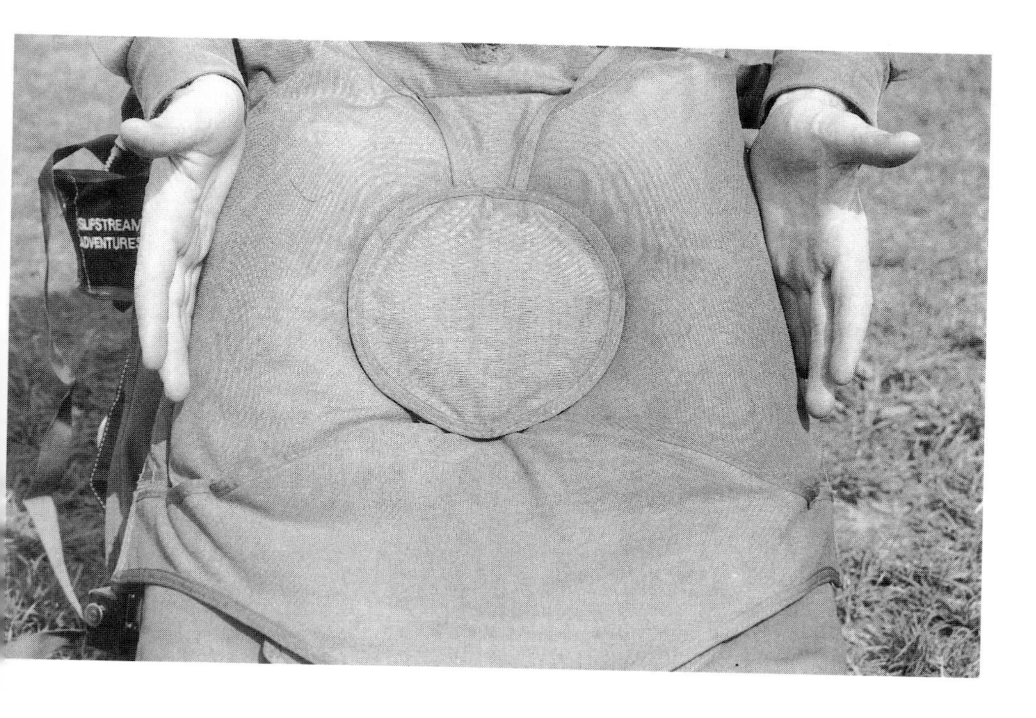

The main canopy is tightly packed into the lower half of the rig. When the ripcord is pulled, the main pin is withdrawn from its retaining loop, and the deployment sequence begins.

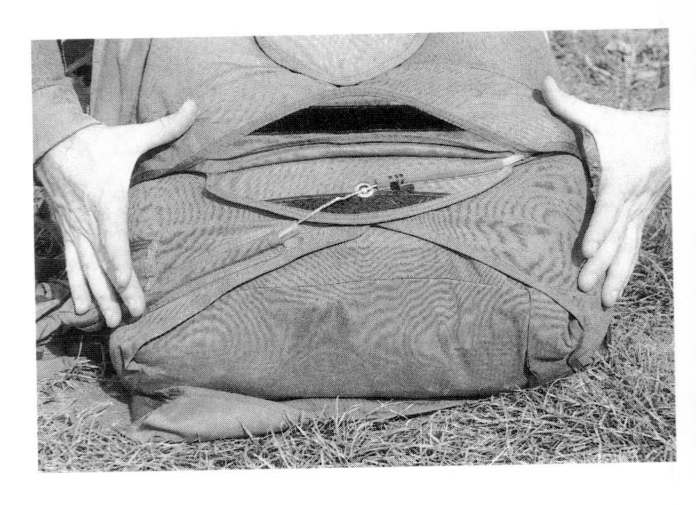

straight on to square parachutes – the sort of rigs that we jump ourselves.'

Our main and reserve parachutes would be stowed 'piggy-back', one above the other on our backs; the main canopy in the bottom of the container, the reserve above it.

On the front of the harness were three handles.

'The main ripcord is made of stainless steel wire and it's housed inside a metal flexi-tube that runs, through the rig, from the container on your back to the Main Ripcord Handle at waist level on the front of your harness.'

The Main Handle itself is simply a 2 in. length of yellow plastic pipe – about the size of a cotton reel, making it easy to see and grab with a gloved hand.

'When you pull your Main Ripcord Handle, the entire length of wire is pulled out of the flexi-tube and comes away in your hand.'

She turned the rig round, and lifted a small flap.

'That pulls out this one pin which is all that's holding the main parachute container closed. As the pin is withdrawn, the tightly-packed container bursts open, a spring-loaded pilot 'chute forces its way out and is opened in the airflow above you. The pilot 'chute then drags a small bag containing the main canopy out of the container on your back. As that bag is pulled off your back, all the rigging lines – which until then have been neatly stowed in the container – straighten out above you; and finally, the canopy is dragged out of its bag and fills with air.'

Throughout the time in freefall, your Main Handle is within easy reach of the Primary Instructor, allowing him to 'dump you out' if for any reason he's unhappy with the dive. An additional handle for the

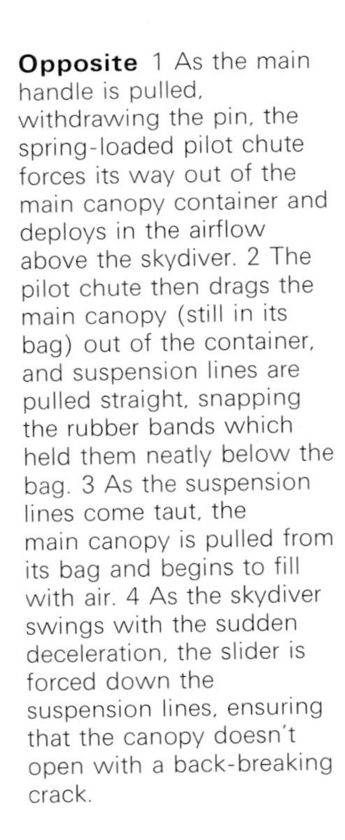

Opposite 1 As the main handle is pulled, withdrawing the pin, the spring-loaded pilot chute forces its way out of the main canopy container and deploys in the airflow above the skydiver. 2 The pilot chute then drags the main canopy (still in its bag) out of the container, and suspension lines are pulled straight, snapping the rubber bands which held them neatly below the bag. 3 As the suspension lines come taut, the main canopy is pulled from its bag and begins to fill with air. 4 As the skydiver swings with the sudden deceleration, the slider is forced down the suspension lines, ensuring that the canopy doesn't open with a back-breaking crack.

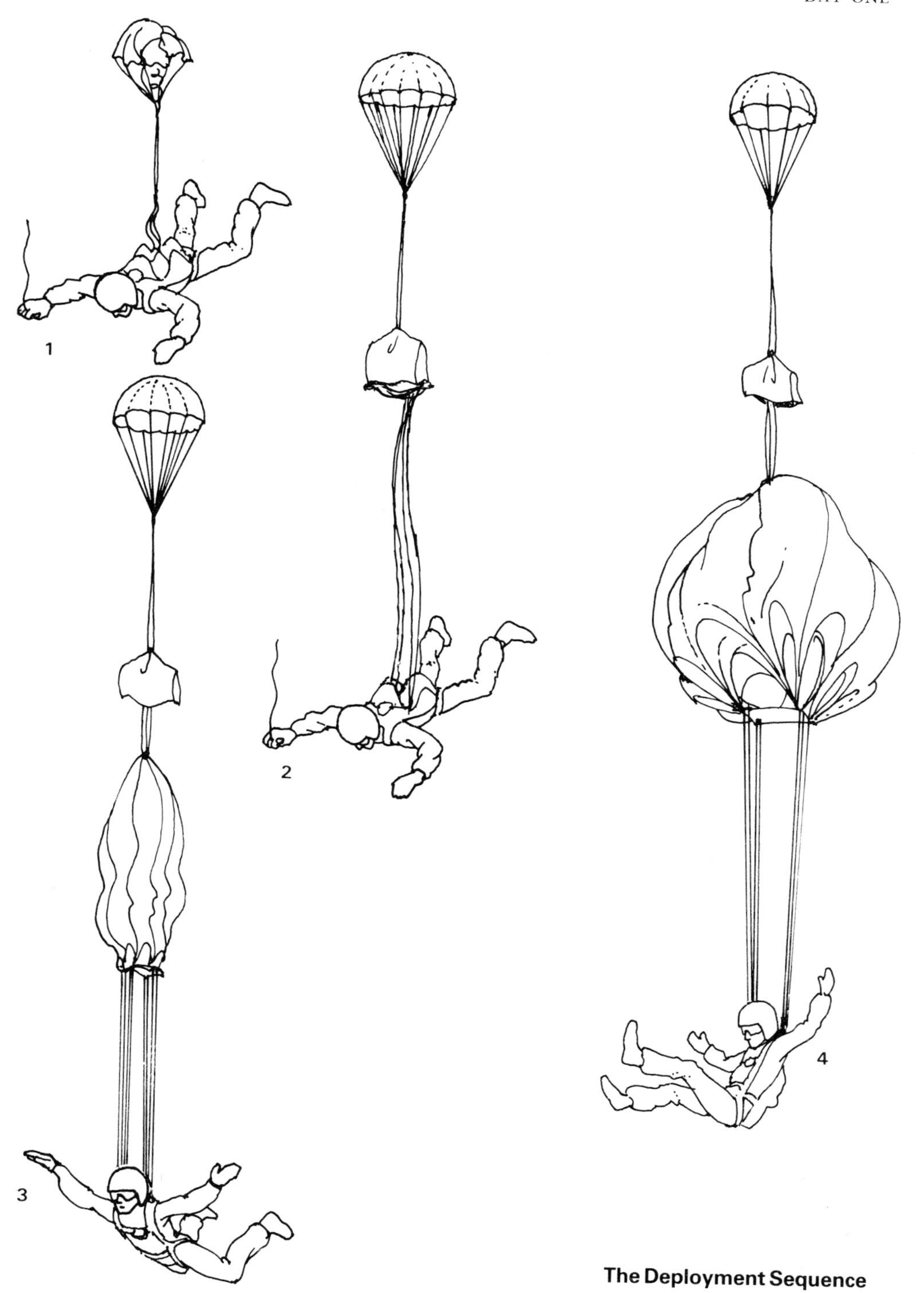

The Deployment Sequence

main parachute is fitted on the opposite side of the rig, giving the Secondary Instructor the same option.

'There are two other handles on your front: on the right hand side is a soft pad or Cut-away Handle which is what you'd use to jettison your main parachute if it ever malfunctioned; and the silver handle on the left-hand side operates your reserve.'

At this stage, it still seemed odd that anyone would ever want to get rid of a main parachute; and the fact that there would be a handle on my chest inviting me to do so was rather unnerving.

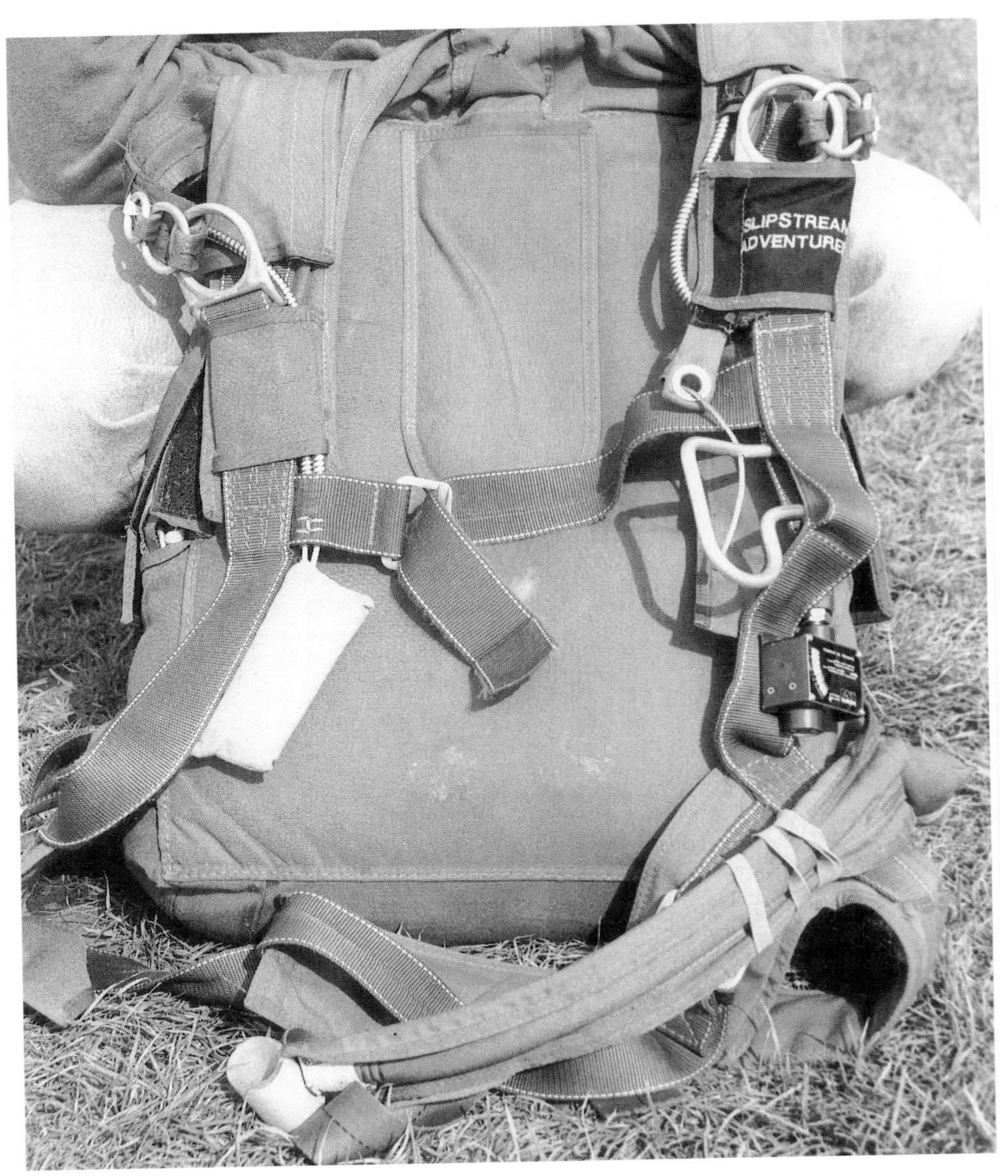

The Accelerated Freefall parachute or rig, showing the relative positions of the three handles: the Main Ripcord Handle, (bottom left) on the belly band; the soft squidgy Cut-away Pad (centre left); and the metal, p-shaped Reserve Handle (centre right). The black box is the Automatic Actuation Device (AAD).

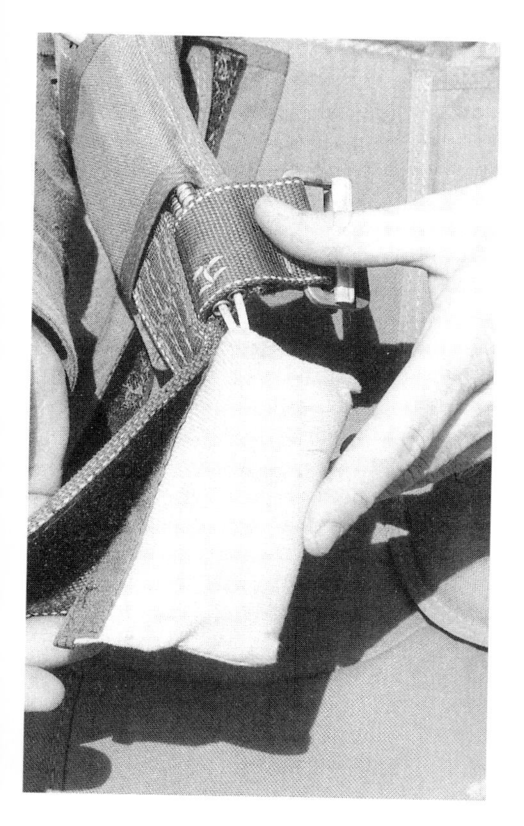

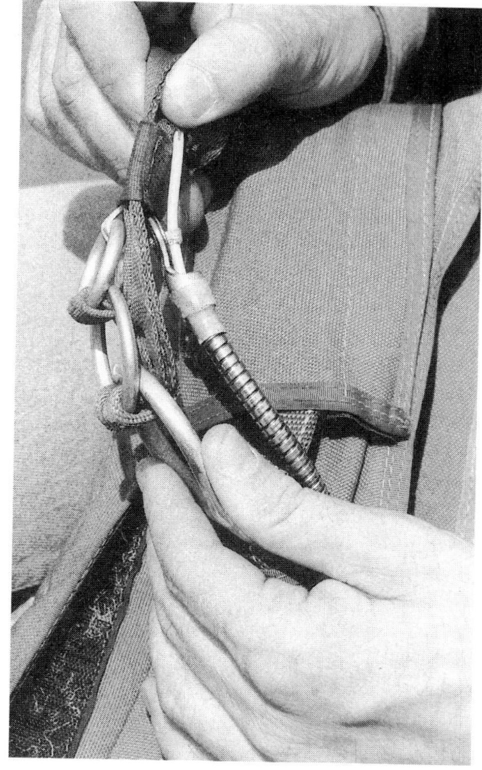

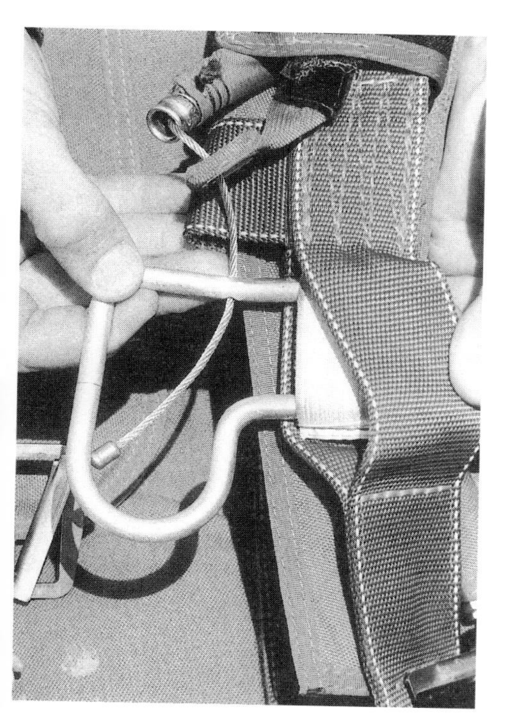

Above left The Cut-away Pad is attached by a strip of Velcro to the righthand side of the harness, just below the chest band.

Above Each of the wires from the Cut-away Pad is led through the harness to a Main Parachute attachment point (or Three Ring Circus) on the skydiver's shoulders. As the Cut-away Pad is pulled, the wires are withdrawn from their retaining loops, the rings disengage from each other and the skydiver is released from his malfunctioning main canopy.

Left The Reserve Handle is retained by an elastic sleeve in the harness on the left side of the skydiver's chest. The tape which is attached to the wire ripcord, between the handle and the metal flexitube, is known as the Stephens Lanyard. If the main parachute has to be cut-away as the result of a malfunction, the departing canopy tightens the lanyard, pulling the Reserve Handle with it.

'Can't you just deploy your reserve as soon as you see the main canopy fluttering uselessly above you?'

'Well you could,' said Jane, 'but there's a chance that they'd get entangled. So you have to "cut" the main away. We'll go through what we call the Cut-away Drills later on.'

The AFF student rigs are fitted with another crucial safety feature: a small pressure-operated device which fires your reserve parachute for you at a pre-selected altitude.

'It's called an Automatic Actuation Device (AAD); it works on barometric pressure and rate of descent. And the theory is that, if you're going through 1,500 ft and there still isn't a parachute above your head, it'll fire your reserve for you.'

There's little point in learning how the AAD works. 'I know they do work,' said Jane. 'I've seen them work. But obviously, it is only a back up; we can't guarantee it's going to work. We'll set it for you just before we get into the aircraft; and then the best thing is just to ignore it totally. As far as you're concerned it doesn't exist. If you need to use your reserve, you pull it for yourself.'

With an instructor either side of you, it's extremely unlikely that your AAD will ever be put to the test.

The Invisible Friend: in theory, the Automatic Actuation Device or AAD, operated by barometric pressure, will deploy your reserve parachute at a predetermined altitude, if for any reason you fail to do so. In practice, you quickly learn to forget about it.

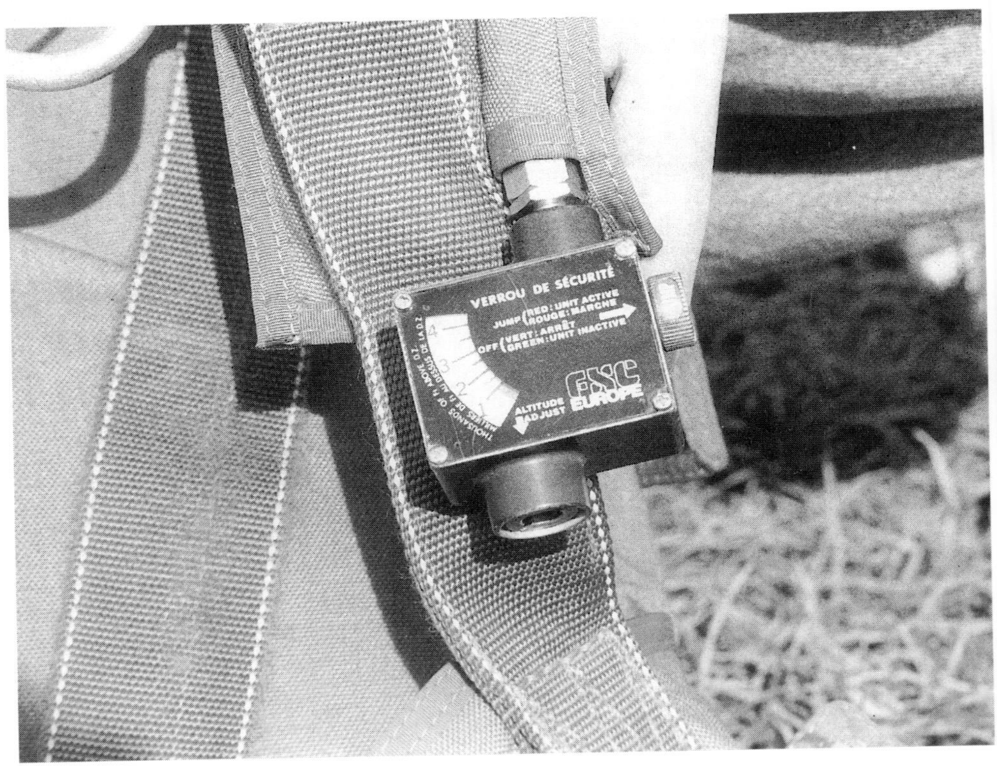

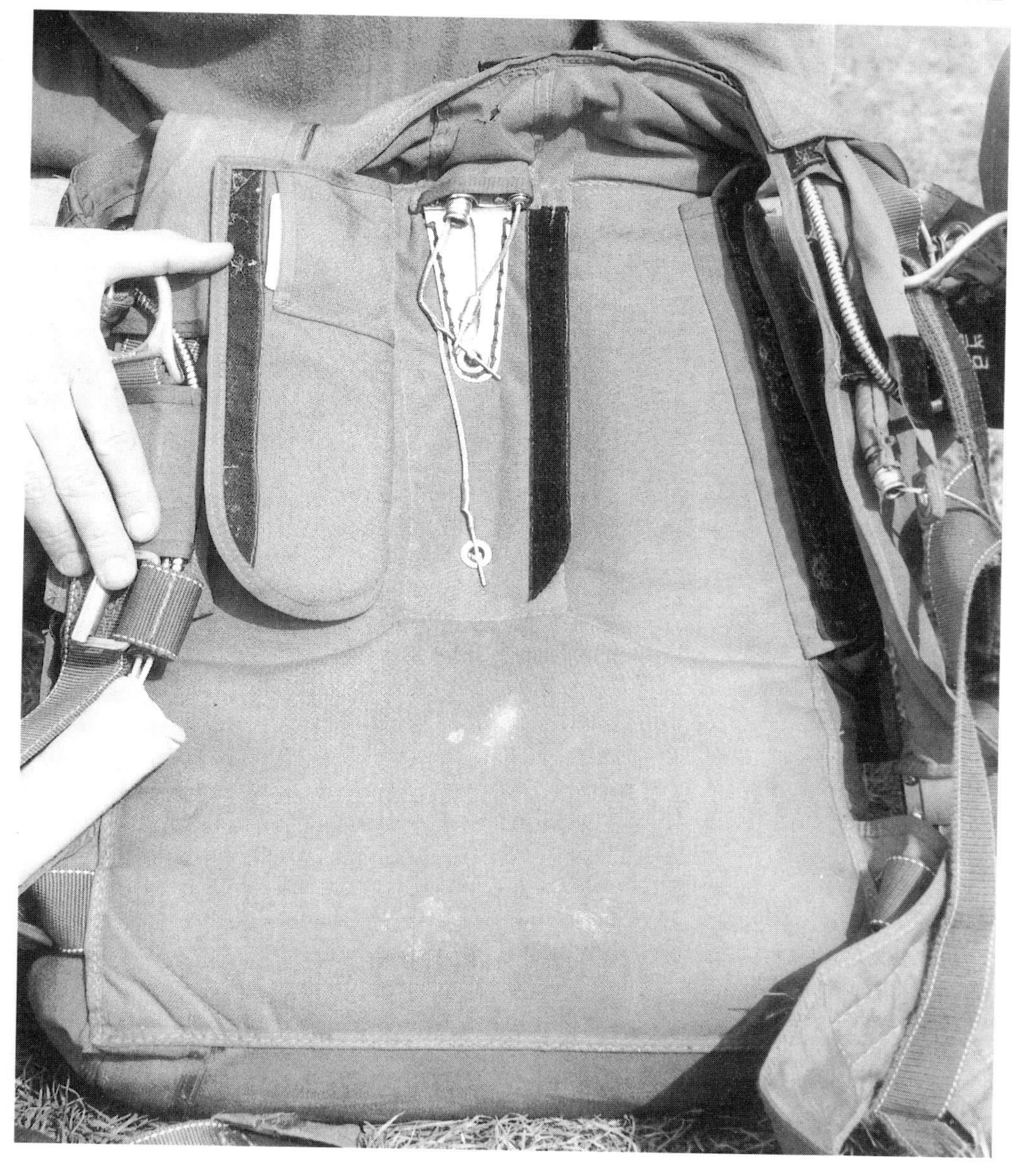

'But if you did end up relying on it,' said Jane, 'we'd probably suggest politely that parachuting isn't your sport.'

A final safety feature on the student rigs is the Stephens Lanyard, a narrow tape which links the main parachute to the Reserve Handle. If for some reason you *are* forced to cut-away your main parachute, the departing canopy will tighten the lanyard, until it automatically pulls the Reserve Handle with it.

Wire ripcords from the Reserve Handle and the Automatic Actuation Device arrive at the same pins (for the Reserve parachute), housed under a flap on the inside of the rig.

'Again,' she said, firmly, 'I've told you it exists, but it is only a back-up; you mustn't rely on it. We'll teach you the same cut-away drills that you'll use when you buy your own parachute. But even in the unlikely event of a malfunction, we'd still expect you to pull the Reserve yourself, not just let the Stephens Lanyard do it for you.

'What we're saying is that there's no way that you won't end up under a parachute.'

When she'd finished, it all seemed so stunningly logical. There wasn't a single stitch or square inch of fabric that didn't perform some useful function in delivering the wearer safely to the ground. By the time you've learnt *why* each part of a rig has been designed as it has, your confidence is complete. According to one AFF student who'd graduated shortly before me, all her fears had evaporated as soon as she'd been shown the equipment in detail.

'People aren't blindly trusting that it's all going to work,' she said. 'You're taught how the canopy works; you know about it; it's not just, "Yes, I think I've got the hang of that." You really understand it.'

Effectively, you're leaving the aircraft with a fail-safe parachute system and two human life insurance policies – an instructor on either side of you. Add to that your own reactions and finally, the pressure-operated AAD as a back-up, and you're well covered.

From that first morning on, you're expected to check your own equipment before each jump. Naturally, it takes some time to work out exactly what you're checking; but it soon becomes instinctive.

Steve and I took it in turns to try on a rig. With all straps and loops tightened up, you feel well on your way to an impression of Harry Houdini. But the reassuring thing is that the most vital parts of the rig – the Main Ripcord Handle, the Cut-away Pad and the Reserve Handle – are all within easy reach. What did concern me slightly was the fact that the Main Handle and the Cut-away Pad were only 10 in. to 12 in. apart; and I was still unhappy about the possibility of jettisoning my main parachute by mistake. Fortunately, the drills for the pull are very clear and simple – in every case, you're taught to look down, to *see* exactly where you're putting your hand.

'No one at Headcorn has ever pulled the Cut-away Pad by mistake,' said Jane. 'Richard Branson who did his AFF course at Netheravon is the only person I know of who's managed it. And anyway, the two handles are designed to feel completely different. The

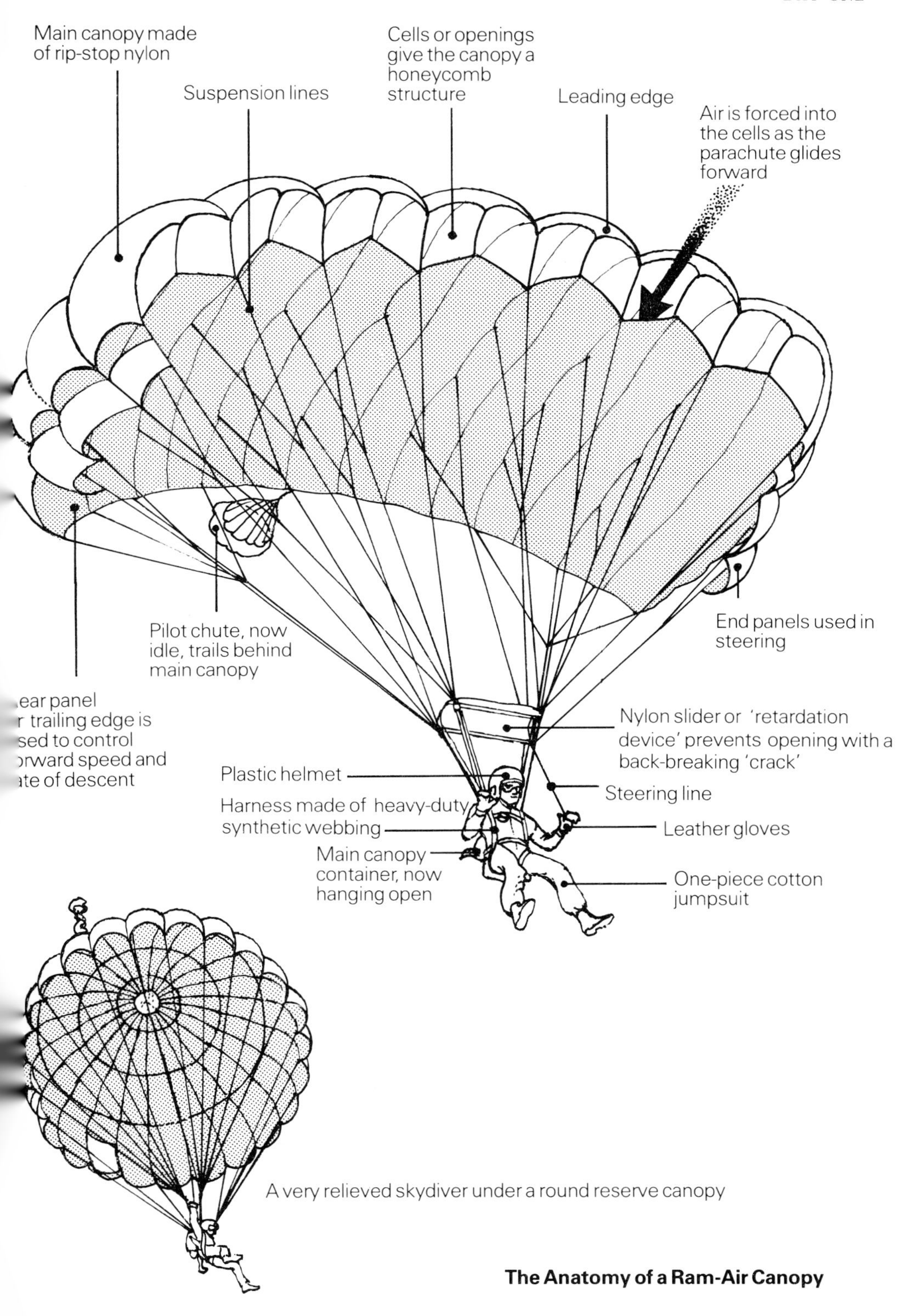

The Anatomy of a Ram-Air Canopy

Cut-away Pad is soft and squidgy, and the Main Handle is metal.'

'In any case,' she said, 'during the first jump, you actually go through the motions of pulling the Main Handle three times, by slapping your hand onto the handle while we're still high. If your hand is going to the wrong handle, the instructor on this side will get hold of your hand and bash it on the correct one. If he still thinks you're going to pull the Cut-away, he'll stop you from grabbing it by holding onto it when you go in for the pull. So don't worry, we'll make sure you pull the right handle.'

Most AFF rigs have a basic, round reserve canopy, designed simply to get you safely onto the ground. It can be steered but it only has limited forward speed. Slipstream have five of these special AFF student rigs.

'We've got one with a very large main parachute which you'll be jumping – we give that to our heaviest people,' said Jane. 'That's 340 square feet, and you could just about land a jeep under it. Then we've got three standard rigs at 300 square feet. And then there's a smaller one which is 250 square feet which we give to six stone women.'

These training rigs cost around £3,000 ($5,100) each. But to buy your own rig, you're looking at around £1,500 to £1,800 ($2,500–$3,000), depending on whether you buy a square or a round reserve.

I'd like to meet the person who designed the harness for the AFF rigs: I'd be able to tell him, in a very high voice, how comfortable I found them. Strength and security have swept style and comfort firmly to one side. And flamboyance is reserved instead for the parachutes and jumpsuits, generally matching, with patterns to suit everyone from the horticulturalist to the Hawaiian beach bum.

When it comes to putting on the harness, experienced jumpers seem to slip into them as effortlessly as most people put on a bathrobe. But for the first timers – or maybe just tall first timers – you feel strung up like a joint of pork.

Next came the altimeter; a small pressure-calibrated dial which registers your altitude and rate of descent. It slides easily onto the chest band, a foot or so below your chin; and there you can watch its bright orange hand sweeping confidently round the dial.

'On your first jump – and that should be this evening if the weather improves – we'll be going to 12,000 ft; so by the time we leave the plane, the hand on the altimeter should be back to the 12 o'clock position.

Countdown to the pull: at 120mph, the hand on an altimeter will sweep through 6,000ft in 30 seconds.

'Now, for the first few seconds after we've left the aircraft,' said Jane, 'we won't be dropping very fast. At first, we'll be falling with almost the same forward speed as the aircraft – about 70 mph. By the time we reach terminal velocity, which is about 12 seconds after exit, we'll be falling at 120 mph. And we won't go any faster than that unless we alter our body position. At 120 mph, we'll be falling at roughly 200 ft a second.'

An hour later – in the early afternoon of the first day – Steve and I took it in turns to climb into another harness, this time suspended from the rafters in the packing shed. It was time to be introduced to the Cut-away Drills – the business of dealing with canopy malfunctions.

Steve, my partner on the course, was wearing his undertaker expression.

'How easy is it to recognise a malfunction?'

'Very easy,' said Jane, 'If it's not the right shape, it's the wrong shape. It's as simple as that. It's very obvious.'

The main parachute, we learnt, can either malfunction *totally* – the ripcord is dangling from your hand and there's definitely something missing overhead – or *partially*. The canopy may leave the container but remains in its bag above your head (*bag lock*); a rigging line may get caught over the top of the canopy (*line over*); the steering lines could become tangled (*tangled steering lines*); or the canopy may fail to inflate (*streamer*). There are also several 'unusual parachute openings' which don't necessarily require that you cut-away and pull your reserve. None, if left unattended, is conducive to long life and happiness; but fortunately, all of them are very rare. I wondered how many times Jane had had to deal with a malfunction in 3,070 jumps?

'Look, Reach, Pull': practising the pull sequence and Cut-away Drills in the packing shed at Headcorn.

'Well, I've cut-away a square parachute twice,' she said. 'But if I'd had the experience then that I have now, I wouldn't have got rid of them. When anyone has a "reserve ride", it's normally human error and very rarely equipment failure. When it comes to the safety records of the equipment, that seems to say it all.'

For an hour, we practised the Cut-away Drills: again and again, we counted our way through a canopy deployment; Jane would call out a type of malfunction, and we'd have to react in the appropriate sequence for each.

For the first few jumps, a small one-way radio is strapped to your harness.

'It's really just so that another instructor can talk to you from the ground when you're under the canopy,' said Jane, 'just in case you're making a real cock-up of it. We don't plan to talk to you, but it's there if we need to tell you which way to turn.'

Next was the jump suit, a one piece outfit with a zip from crutch to throat. Just when you've got used to the number of handles on the harness, the grips on this jump suit – one on each arm and thigh – suddenly brings the total number of handles dangling around you to seven. Leather gloves, a pair of goggles and a lightweight helmet complete the uniform. And although some students smile at the idea of a

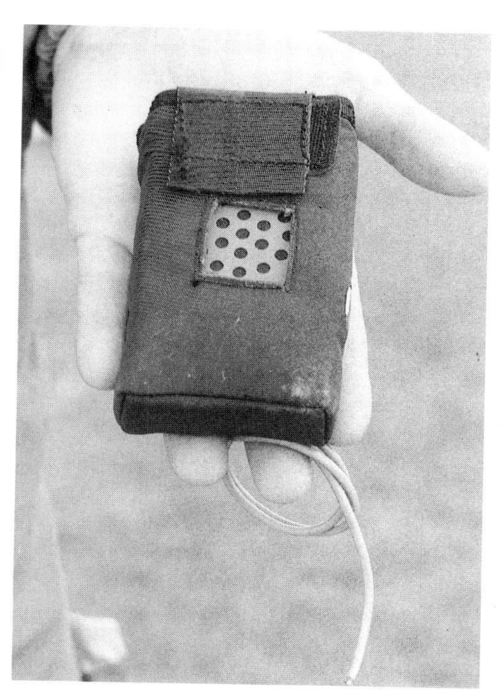

Above left For the first jump or two, a small one-way radio is fitted to your harness. 'The instructors on the ground may not need to talk to you', said Jane, 'but it's there in case we see you steering off towards France.'

Above AFF jumpsuits are fitted with handles on thighs and shoulders; initially as grips for the instructors, and later, for use in Relative Work, when human formations are put together in the sky.

Left Helmet, goggle and gloves: under BPA rules, all skydivers must wear a helmet (as opposed to a lightweight frappe cap) until they've logged 200 jumps.

lightweight helmet – precious use at stopping a 120 mph ground-induced headache – rules are rules.

The theory is that a helmet provides some protection when leaving the aircraft and in the unlikely event of a collision between two jumpers falling at roughly the same speed. In practice, most jumpers wear them only until they've done the regulation 200 jumps in a hard hat. Most then change to what's called a frappe hat, a simple and very unflattering skull cap.

The goggles should be held on firmly so that they don't ride up over your eyebrows in the windblast – spectacles are fine if you make a strap out of rubber bands which goes round the back of your head; and Jane's recommendation – 'I like everything nice and tight' – is sound advice.

If skydiving involved simply falling out of an aircraft and tumbling for 8,000 ft, life would be very simple. The skill is learning to do so in a controlled manner. The key to that is achieving what's known as the 'Stable Position' – much like a frog in mid-leap, with arms and legs spread; the spine is curved forward in the sort of position you might adopt if you wanted to demonstrate a beer belly, with the stomach pushed forward. Arching the spine is the most important part of the stable position. With your spine curved forwards so that the front of your body is convex – your centre of gravity, the lowest central point in the body, is pushed through to a point in the area of your tummy button. Providing that you achieve that position, you'll fall face-to-earth. In this position, the body falls much like a shuttle cock. By presenting your body to the airflow in a form that is as close to symmetrical as possible, you'll be falling 'down the tube' – in other words, dropping vertically downwards with no lateral, forward or backward movement.

Practising the position on the ground is uncomfortable. But in freefall, the force of the wind tends to force you fairly naturally into the correct position.

'The lower legs are raised roughly 45 degrees from horizontal; by pushing the toes upwards and away from you, your knees are lifted up into the correct position.'

By now Jane was spread-eagled face down on the floor of the Slipstream Office.

'Now, you don't really have to strain to get into this position,' she said. 'As you leave the aircraft, you'll have to concentrate on the position; but as soon as you're flying comfortably you won't really have to think about it anymore. It'll feel completely natural.'

'If you don't achieve the stable position, a lot of turbulence is created below your body, making you very unstable; the air buffets and can't flow smoothly round the curve of the body.'

If you're in a complete 'reverse arch' – in other words when the front of your body is concave – the turbulence can even roll you over on your back. Don't fight the air and you'll find that the stable position is very easy to maintain. Experienced jumpers will leave the aircraft in any old position. Backwards, sideways, even tucked into a canonball. But they, too, will always get back into the stable position for the pull, so that the parachute comes cleanly off their back. For at least the first two levels, Steve and I would each have two instructors using hand signals to help us get into a strong stable position.

By 1100 on Monday, just two hours into the course, Jane talked Steve and me through the first jump.

'We'll leave the aircraft at 12,000 ft and get stable. Then you'll do what's called a 'Circle of Awareness', followed by three 'Practice Pulls' – I'll explain those in a moment – then another Circle of Awareness. After that, you can just enjoy your jump. Stick your tongue out and have a good scream until 5,000 ft.

'At 5,000 ft, you'll be reminded of the altitude, because the instructors will take hold of your arms and shake them; so at that stage, the altitude awareness is coming from them, not from you; we want you just to enjoy it until then.

'Having felt the tug on your arms, you'll turn to the Primary Instructor on your right and shout, "5,000 ft". Then you'll get the Pull Signal, which is simply an index finger pointing straight at the Main Ripcord Handle. And that's when you deploy your parachute. It's unmistakeable, and it's totally different from any other signal you'll get.'

The Circle of Awareness involves simply looking forward and down at the ground, then at the altimeter under your chin, and then turning your head to each instructor and shouting the altitude.

'By comparing how the ground looks at different heights, you begin to develop altitude awareness; you're making a mental note. Experienced jumpers use their altimeters very little, because their altitude awareness is so well developed.

'Now obviously,' said Jane, 'when you shout the altitudes, we don't need them to nearest half inch; the nearest 500 ft is fine. And you still shout the same altitude to both instructors, even though you'll have fallen another 800 ft in the four seconds or so that it takes you to complete the Circle of Awareness.

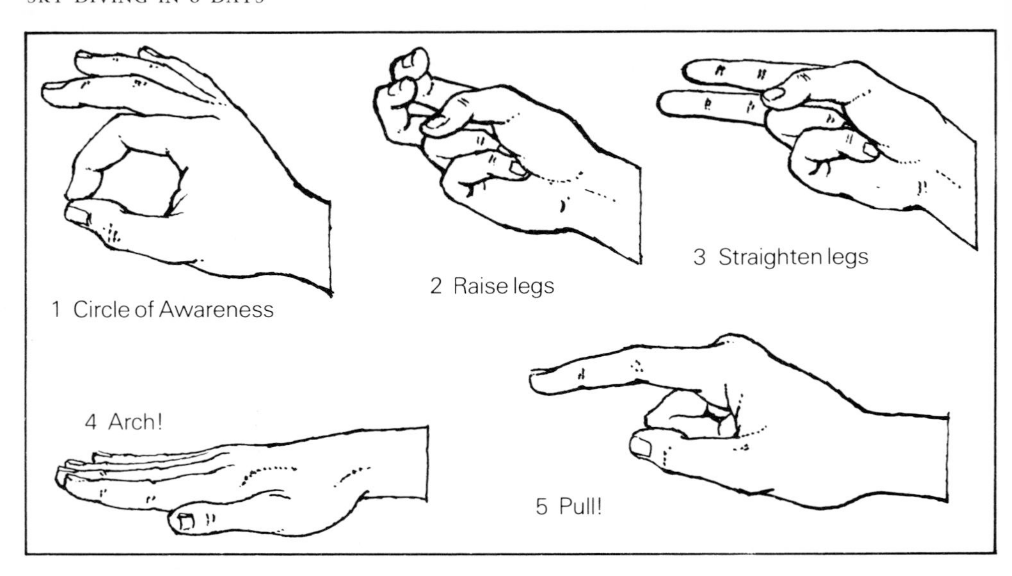

Skydiving handsignals

'Eye contact with the instructors is very important,' she said. 'You should look straight into their eyes, shout the altitude and they'll either give you a thumbs up or some other signal.'

For the Practice Pulls, there are three distinct movements and the sequence is *Look, Reach, Pull* which you shout out as you go through the motions: firstly, moving only your head, you lower your chin and *Look* down at the Main Handle. Secondly, you *Reach* down for it with your right hand and lay the palm of your hand on the Main Handle – at the same time sweeping your left arm above your head, in order to keep your symmetry in the airflow. And finally, you simulate the *Pull*, by simply returning your arms to the stable position.

'After three Practice Pulls and another Circle of Awareness, you go into what we call 'Free Time', or as the Americans call it, Leisure Time: you simply relax, lie on the air and just enjoy yourself. We still want you to be aware, to look at the ground and all around you. You can smile, give us a thumbs up, just have a good time, all right? When you get the Pull Signal itself, the only difference in the *Look, Reach, Pull* sequence is that you grab the handle firmly and pull the ripcord away, withdrawing the pin. And as the parachute deploys you yell out, "*One thousand, two thousand, three thousand, four thousand . . .*', by which time the canopy should have fully opened above you and you can look up and check that it's the right shape.'

So much for the cold, clinical theory. But what does

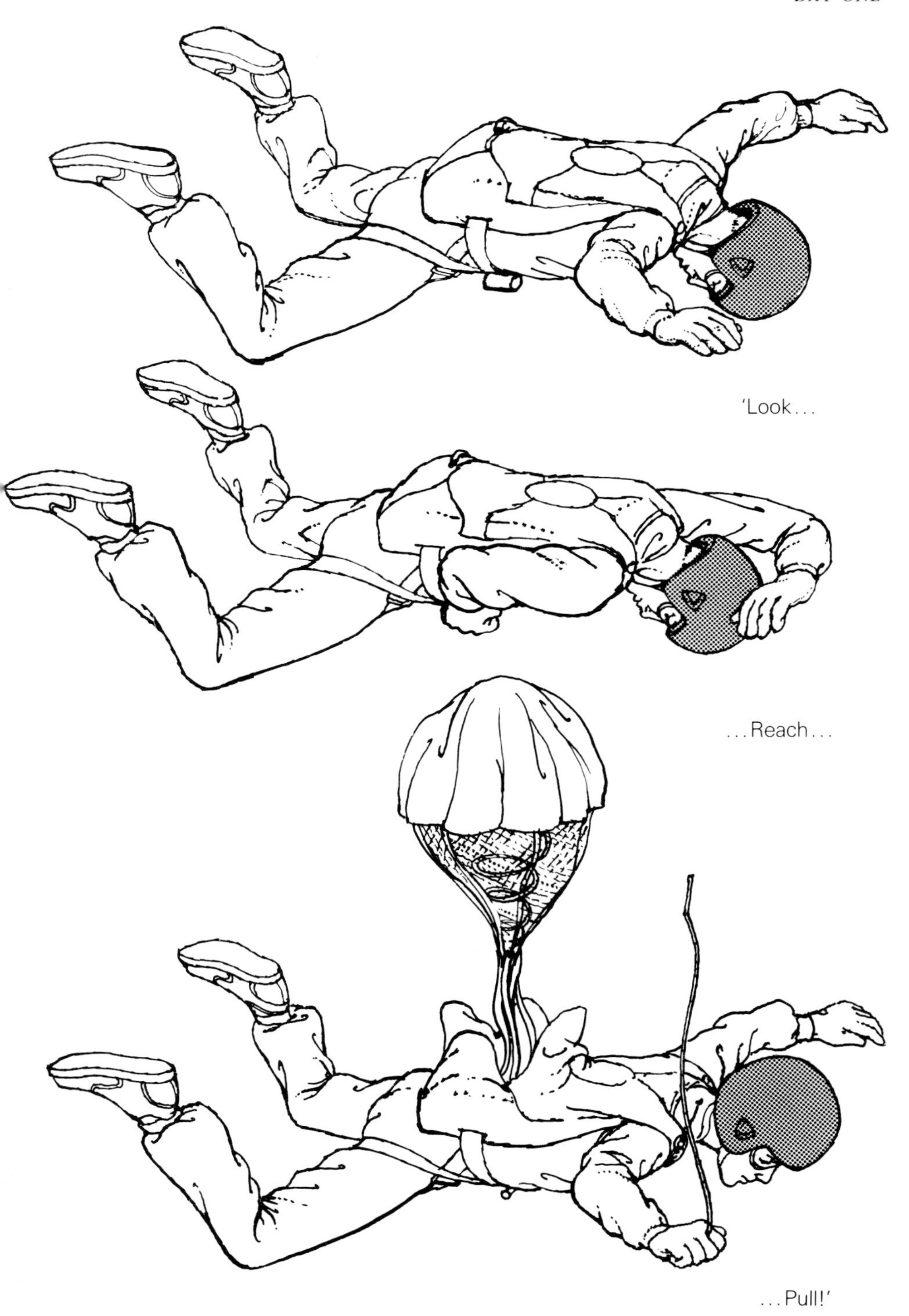

The Pull Sequence

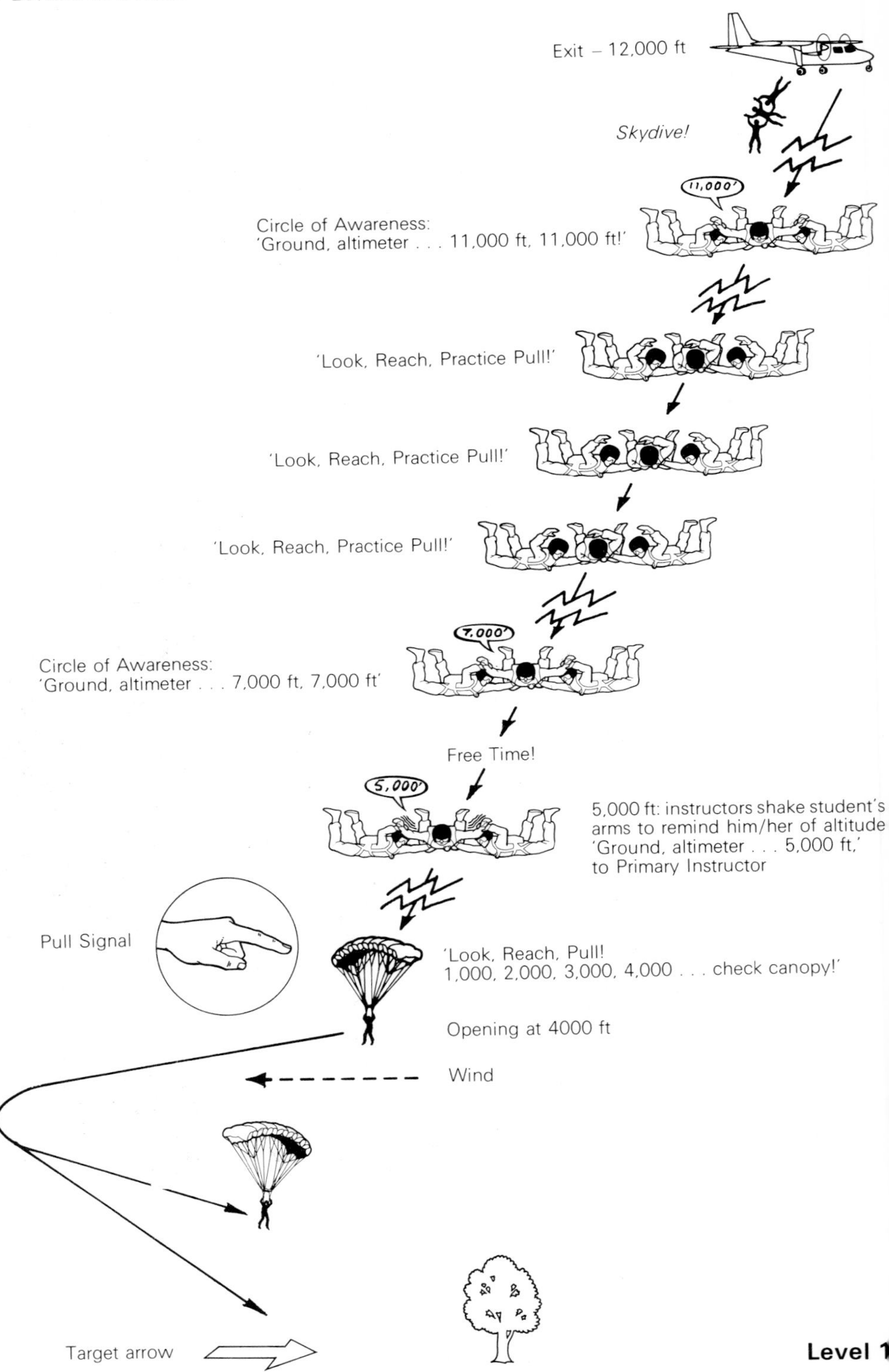
Exit – 12,000 ft
Skydive!
11,000'
Circle of Awareness:
'Ground, altimeter . . . 11,000 ft, 11,000 ft!'
'Look, Reach, Practice Pull!'
'Look, Reach, Practice Pull!'
'Look, Reach, Practice Pull!'
7,000'
Circle of Awareness:
'Ground, altimeter . . . 7,000 ft, 7,000 ft'
Free Time!
5,000'
5,000 ft: instructors shake student's arms to remind him/her of altitude
'Ground, altimeter . . . 5,000 ft,' to Primary Instructor
Pull Signal
'Look, Reach, Pull!
1,000, 2,000, 3,000, 4,000 . . . check canopy!'
Opening at 4000 ft
Wind
Target arrow

Level 1

it really *feel* like when you launch yourself out of an aircraft for the first time?

Jane smiled. 'Well for the first few seconds, you may not be very aware of what's going on, and that's quite normal. The American term for it is "Sensory Overload". When you've left the aircraft, obviously, you're going to be frightened. That's natural, and we accept it. Everything's happening at once and you think, "What the hell am I doing here?" But then, after three or four seconds, you suddenly realise that everything's fine, the instructors are there and you'll think, "Oh well, let's get on with the next bit".

'On the way up in the aircraft, your priority is just to think about what you're going to be doing. At various points on the ascent, we'll be asking you questions about what you'll be doing at each height. We'll point out the airfield and the landing point which is in the area of a large white arrow.'

By mid-afternoon, we were sitting in an aircraft mock-up, a blue wooden fuselage with an open door

Stage 2 of the exit procedure: hanging from the doorway of the wooden mock-up, Rod Bartholomew (the Secondary Instructor) and Jane Buckle (Primary), talk me through the Hotel Check:
'Check In', to Jane.
'Okay', . . .

'Check out', to Rod.
'Okay'.

onto a paved patio. Every parachute jump is practised in rehearsals known as 'dirt dives'.

'Right, when it's time for your jump,' said Jane, 'the Secondary Instructor will take hold of your leg strap, put his face up to yours and shout, "*Are you ready to skydive?*"

'If you say, "*Ready!*" you'll be told to put your legs out after him. When you're in the door on the lefthand side of the aircraft, facing forward you'll do what's called a "Hotel Check". That is: you put your hands – one on top of the other – at the very edge of the door, beside your leg. Then you look in at the Primary Jumpmaster and say, "*Check in.*" If he's quite happy

Exit Procedure on Levels 1 to 3

Secondary Instructor:
'Are you ready to skydive'?
Student (involuntarily)
'Ready'!
Secondary Instructor:
'Then put your legs out after me'!

with everything, he'll say, "*Okay*." Then you look out at the Secondary, who'll be hanging out of the door and you say, "*Check Out*." He'll reply, "*Okay*."'

Leaving the aircraft is like compressing your body into a spring: you look forward along the aircraft heading, lean forward with some weight on your hands, push yourself *up* with your hands, lower yourself *down* again, and finally you *push* yourself out of the aircraft, shouting '*Arch!*' as you fall away. So it's, '*Up, Down . . . Arch!*' And away you go.

There's something unnerving about being taught about canopy control – the business of steering and landing a parachute – by an instructor who limps in to give the lesson. But Andy Ring, black-bearded and economical with his facial expressions, has more than 2,000 jumps to his credit.

'In some ways,' he told us, in his quiet, measured

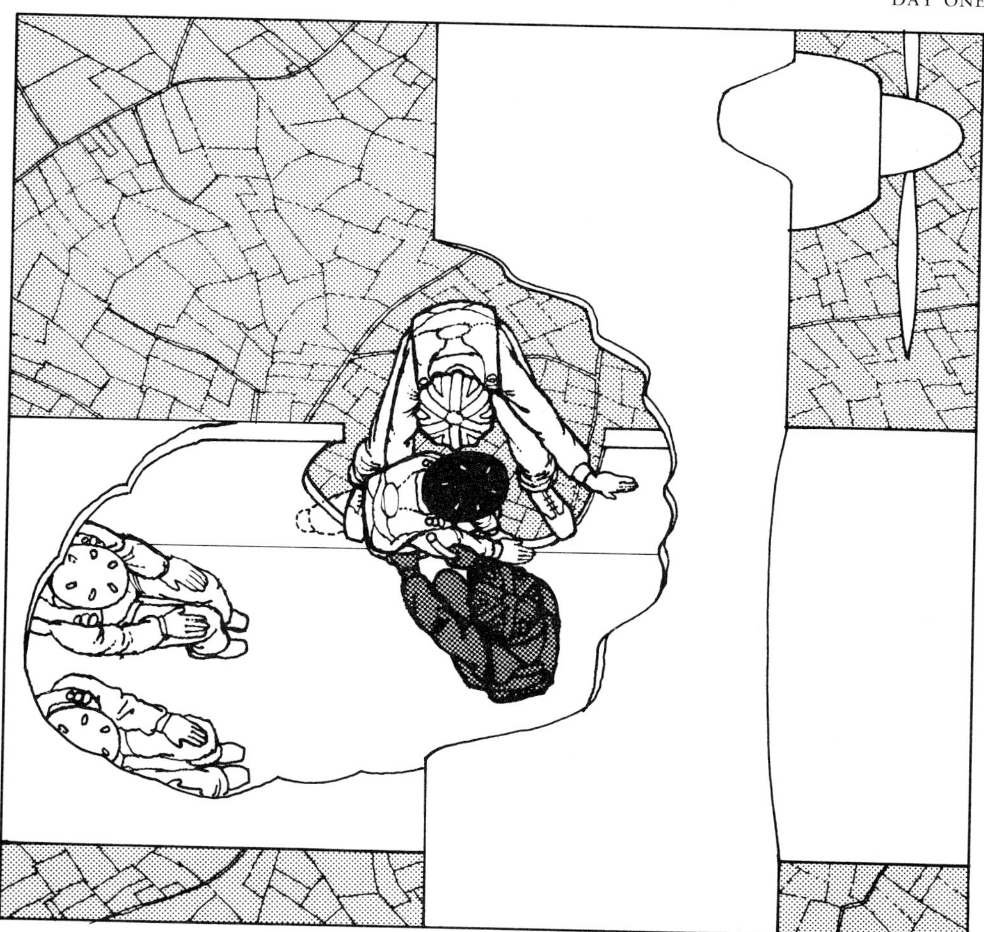

voice, 'this is the most difficult lesson for you, because it's the only one that you can't practise until you're actually gliding around under the parachute. Everything else we can simulate. The object of the exercise is to get you safely from the point where your parachute opens, down to the drop zone avoiding all obstacles *en route*.

'The most important thing to remember is the difference between *ground* speed and *air* speed. Now, even on a completely still day, the square parachutes which you'll be using wouldn't float vertically downwards. Until you begin to modify their shape, they're designed to glide forwards over the ground at roughly 20 mph, as well as downwards. So obviously, if you're going directly into a 10 mile an hour wind, your speed over the ground will be reduced to around 10 mph. Turn 180 degrees and you'll be doing 30 mph.' Landing is almost always done into the wind.

The Hotel Check:
Student (to Primary):
'Check in'!
Primary:
'Okay'!
Student (to Secondary):
'Check out'!
Secondary:
'Okay'!
Student:
'Up, down. . . .

. . . *AAAAAaaaaaaarrchhh!*

Before long we were on to Obstacle Avoidance: 'If the angle between you and an object is staying absolutely constant, you're going to land on it. Now, we don't really mind if you don't land on the white arrow on the airfield. In fact it'd be fine if you landed in the same field.

'Along the rear lower edge of the canopy is a rectangular panel of cloth, made of the same ripstop nylon as the rest of the parachute. Lines from the

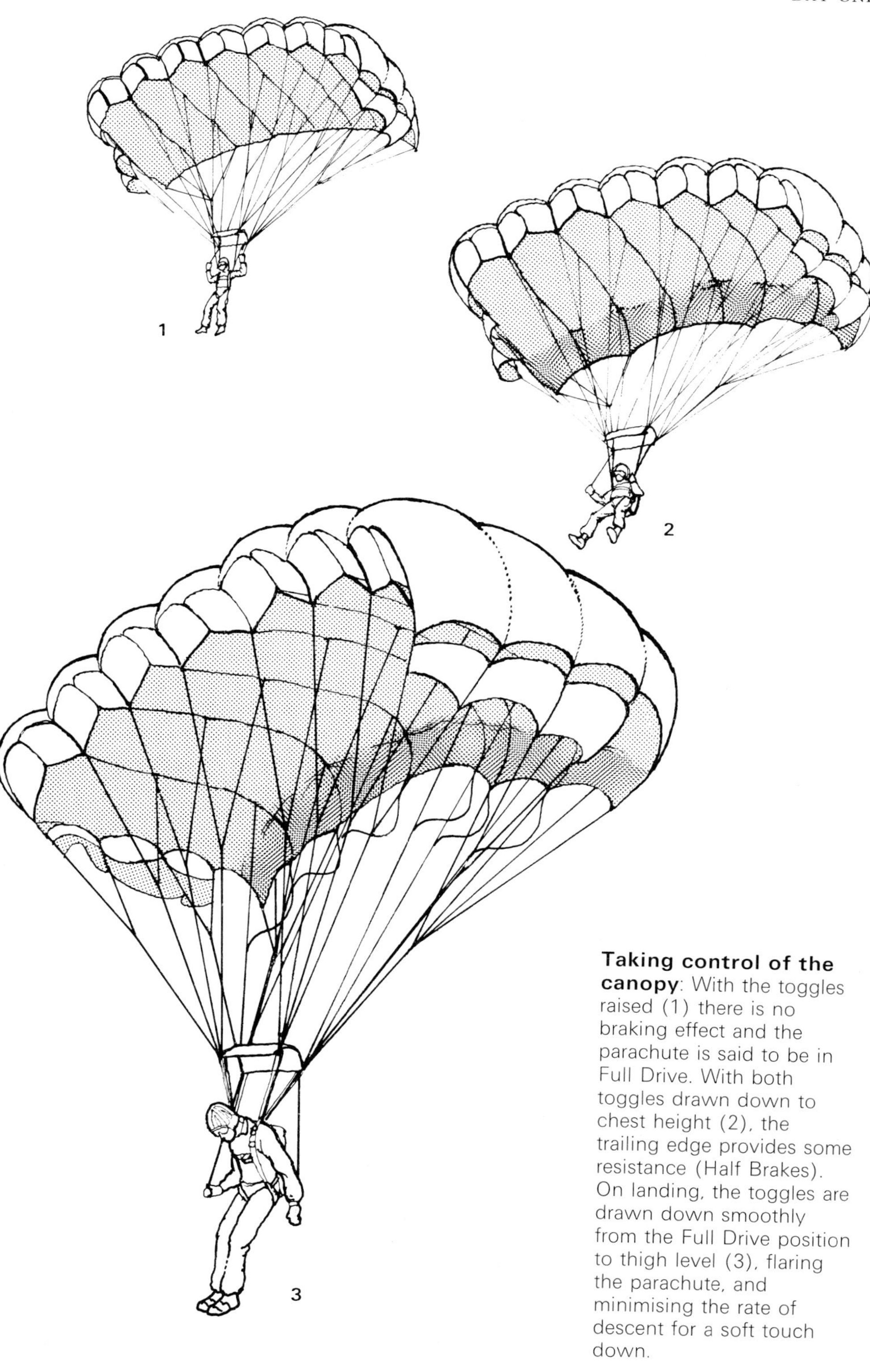

Taking control of the canopy: With the toggles raised (1) there is no braking effect and the parachute is said to be in Full Drive. With both toggles drawn down to chest height (2), the trailing edge provides some resistance (Half Brakes). On landing, the toggles are drawn down smoothly from the Full Drive position to thigh level (3), flaring the parachute, and minimising the rate of descent for a soft touch down.

bottom of this panel are led down to two steering handles or toggles above your head. By taking hold on these handles, you can control how much the panel is drawn down at the rear, which acts likes a brake on the parachute's forward movement. With the toggles raised as high as they'll go, there's no braking effect – the parachute is said to be in *Full Drive*; if you pull them down to waist level or *Half Brakes*, the forward movement is greatly reduced; and if you draw them down until they're level with your thighs, *Full Brakes*, your forward movement is minimal.'

Steering is a simple variation; by only hauling down the left toggle, the left rear corner of the panel is drawn down, creating resistance, and the parachute banks to the left. Draw down on the right and it banks to the right.

'Now, providing there are no obstacles in the way, at 200 ft you allow the parachute to go into Full Drive. You adopt the Parachuting Landing Fall (PLF) position, which we'll teach you later on. And then at 10 ft–15 ft, you do what's called a flare – that means simply drawing the steering toggles smoothly down to their lowest Full Brakes position, so that at the moment your feet touch the floor, downward and forward movement have been reduced as much as possible, giving you the softest possible landing. You should even be able to stand up on your first landing.'

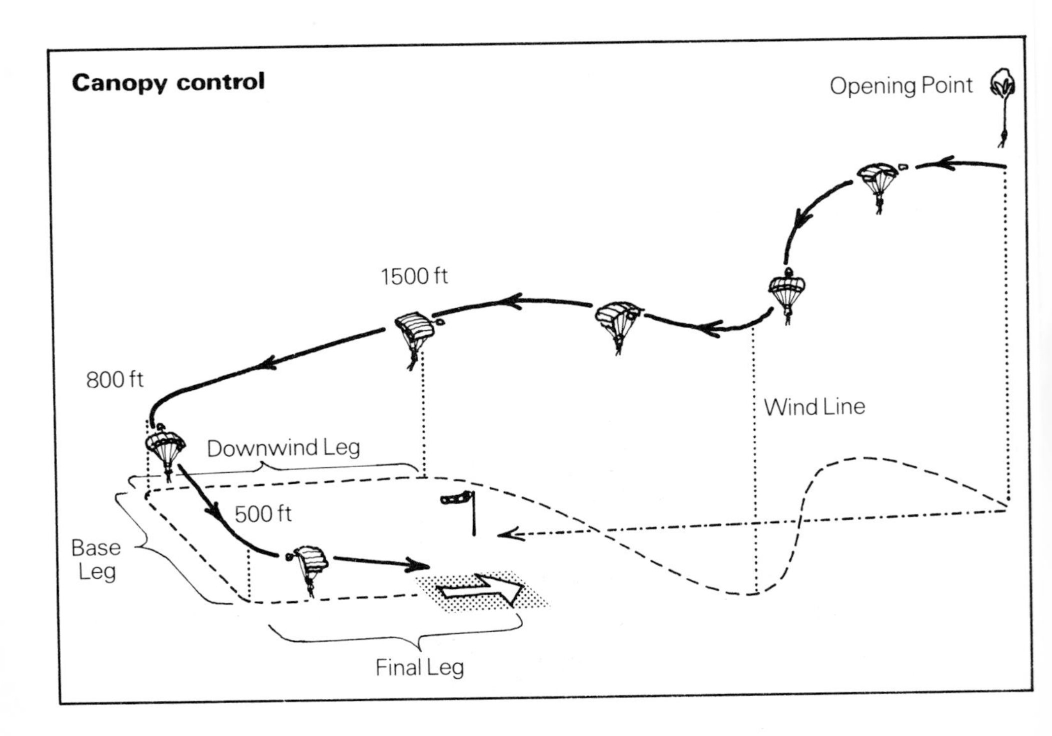

So how did Andy do his back in?

'Well . . . I injured it slightly under a parachute,' he said. 'I had an attack of incompetence on a very high performance rig. I seem to remember I was thinking about work, and mixing the two is definitely not a good idea. I just turned a little bit low – and that's one of the reasons we teach you to turn into wind at 500 ft; if you do turn the parachute low, it will drop you onto the floor pretty hard.'

Is there a record for the furthest distance anyone's ever landed from the Drop Zone? 'Well, we don't seem to have too much trouble with AFF students,' he said, 'but my own personal record is four miles.'

Steve and I practised the landing position and completed a 15 minute written exam; and by 1800 we were fully prepared. The wind was well within the 15 knot limit and only the cloud cover was preventing us from being taken up to the minimum jump altitude of 9,000 ft.

Strangely there isn't a constant preoccupation with whether or not your parachute is going to open. It becomes a calculated and meticulously checked assumption. In the end, you either trust it or you don't. If you're one of the few who don't, things will just be miserable until the canopy billows over your head for the first time.

Steve was feeling much the same. 'My only worry is that I might cock it up,' he said.

And on the AFF course, cocking it up is more than just a dent to the pride. It's a dent to the bank account.

The cloud didn't lift. And two and a half hours later, we packed it in for the day. Understandably, the drop zone is also a dry zone. 'Alcohol and parachuting just don't mix,' says Jane. 'But we do go to the pub in the evening.'

We did.

Miles Clark (left) with Stephen Saberi: Six hours after arriving at Headcorn, we were ready to get our knees in the breeze.

- Jack Gregory: 61 hours in freefall
- First impressions
- Dirt diving in the daisies
- Level 1
- The four second blitz
- Partying on Cloud 9
- Dangling in the sunlit silence
- Preparing for Level 2
- Where's the effing ripcord?

DAY TWO

The television was on in the corner: '. . . *So today's weather chart is quite straightforward. . . . Mainly sunny and dry in the southwest and southeast. That'll be the scene for tomorrow as well, but come Thursday, ugly weather coming across from Scandinavia. . .*'

It was only 7.30, but I was already spread-eagled, face down on the bed, looking left and right, shouting my altitude to the wardrobe and the sink. I explained the equipment checks to the soap dish and whispered the Cutaway Drills to the mirror through a faceful of shaving foam.

If you'd written out an order form headed: 'Weather for Tuesday 4th August', the good Lord could scarcely have done a better job. The sun was belting down on the orchards and hedgerows. I must have been slowly making the transformation from whuffo to skydiver, because it occurred to me, as I drove to the airfield, that anyone who wasn't jumping out of aeroplanes on a day like this, must be utterly mad.

There was a new face on the sofa in the Slipstream office. New to me, that is; but very familiar to the residents of Skid Row.

If the skydiving world was to search among it's pioneers for a leading light, this quiet sandy-haired Californian would rank high among the contenders. In the last 12 of his 31 years on and above planet Earth, Jack Gregory has spent a mind-boggling 61 hours – two and a half days – in freefall. As one of the first ten people in the world to be licenced as an AFF Instructor, he was chosen to join the US Parachute Association's three man training team. In 1981, the team – which included Mike Johnston, now the USPA's Director of Training – toured 15 American drop zones, running the first formal AFF Instructor Courses.

In the last six years, Jack has been living and working at Zephyr Hills, near Tampa, Florida – the centre of the known skydiving world – as well as helping to set up AFF programmes in France, Sweden, Norway and Denmark. Now, he'd come to spend a month or so working for Slipstream, where his first job would be to take over the remainder of Steve's training. Jane would continue with mine.

We were being taught by two of the most experienced skydivers in the world; from our point of view, this personalised tuition was equivalent to having a week's tennis coaching with Ivan Lendl or doing a motor-racing course with Alain Prost. Viewed like that, the cost of the AFF course could be kept in perspective.

Everyone reacts differently to their first jump, and even for highly-experienced jumpers, the memory remains clear. I asked more than a dozen skydivers to describe how they felt in those few seconds after they'd pushed off from the aircraft and began pirouetting through the chouds. Many of them couldn't find the words, but Jack Gregory, who has since logged another 4,400 jumps, still remembers it vividly. 'Obviously, it was all static line stuff; round parachute, chest-mounted reserve and so on. I was the last student out and I remember Ron Cordus, my instructor saying, "Okay, sit in the door," and I climbed out onto the edge. He shouted "Go!", 'and I looked up at him and said,

"Did you say 'Go'?"

"Yes!"

'Oh,' I said, and let go. I forgot all about arching but I seemed to remain basically stable. But, boy, I was scared before the parachute opened. Scared and excited, you know. I kinda liked it. And the first thing I realised was how quiet it was, after all the noise of the aircraft and the wind.'

But when it comes to describing what it *feels* like to curve away from an aircraft into freefall, he throws up his hands. 'How can you describe the indescribable? How can you describe ecstasy? It's more feeling than word, more an emotion than a motion. We sometimes use the term 'airgasm', I guess to try to relate it to sexual pleasures. And after 12 years, it's just getting better.

'One of the first things that awed me about skydiving was that I wasn't touching *anything* solid. You know, we can stand on the ground and jump up in the air and come right back down. But to be out there for a minute at a time – when maybe the only other thing you touch is another human being who's doing the same thing – is just unreal.'

Among skydiving's other international nomads is Pete Gannaw, a 5 ft 5 in. Canadian with a striking resemblance to Elton John. He was spending a few days at Headcorn, a break from coaching part of the West German freefall team. Like everyone who learnt to skydive before the advent of AFF, Pete had started the slow way. He, too, had a clear memory of his first day on an airfield. Could he remember experiencing Sensory Overload?

'Oh yeah, you betcha! I made three static line jumps my first day and even when I was done, I couldn't figure out what the hell was goin' on. I mean, I knew that I'd been in an aeroplane for a little while, and that after that I was under a parachute; but I still couldn't figure out what the heck was happenin'.

'But you know,' he said, 'I've seen people make their first jump looking back at the aeroplane, wavin' at you, lookin' you right square in the eye, and saying, "Hey, I'm havin' a helluva good time; goin' for a parachute ride now, bye."'

Had anything else ever given him the same kind of thrill?

'Well,' he said, 'I dabbled in other sports at school. But I was always the fat blotchy kid that got picked last. I'm not even that good a skydiver. I've got a lot of experience, sure; but as far as talent goes, not much.'

For a man with 2,693 jumps in his logbook, he also has a unlikely admission: 'I'm just petrified of heights,' he said. 'I'm 5 ft 5½ ins and . . . wait a minute . . . that should be 5 ft 5¾ ins. And when my head is more than 8 ft above what's hard, I don't like it!'

Like Jack, Pete is forthright but unpretentious. It's a lesson that they both learnt a long time ago. 'There are some really big egos in this sport,' he says. 'You've really gotta really watch yourself.'

Does that mean that there are wrong reasons for entering the sport?

'Oh yeah,' he said, 'To impress your buddies. But those guys go away real quick.'

Jane Buckle gave up trying to put the freefalling feeling into words a long time ago. 'I just can't describe it,' she says. 'You have to do it. People often

Waiting for Sky: California's own Jack Gregory (left) with Pete Gannaw, coach of the West German freefall team. A pioneer of AFF with almost 5,000 jumps in his log book, Gregory was the chief architect in 1987 of a 126-man star over Belgium, until recently the largest skydiving formation in history.

ask me that. But I just say that I'll ask them the same question when they've done their first jump. And they usually say exactly the same, "I just can't describe it". There's just a feeling of freedom, the feeling of flight.'

As Pete Gannaw admits, 'When it comes right down to it, it cannot be explained exactly; it's totally unique. There are many things that are similar. It's motion; you're moving and controlling your body. It's a bit like the way you learnt to walk a long time ago; you have the balance thing. But like skating and skiing, you're using your body differently. It's direct body control.

'In fact, the body position, and the way you orientate yourself relative to gravity, are similar to scuba diving. But obviously the pace is different; the speed is, well . . . fish speed as opposed to hawk speed!'

'The odd thing,' says Chris Francis, Chief Instructor at Headcorn, 'is that you don't have to be fit to enjoy it. It's relaxation. It's like being on top of the world and you just think, 'Why didn't I start doing this years ago?'

As it turned out, I didn't have to wait long to find out for myself. At 0915, there was a call on the tannoy. '*Will the following people starting getting their kit on: Clark, Buckle, Bartholomew, Gregory, Saberi, Howard, Kuhle, Schrève and Roberts. 20 minute call.*'

Jane and I were looking at a dog-eared air photograph of the airfield which was taped to the door of one of the packing sheds. Someone had thoughtfully high-lighted the rivers and the railway line, the trees, pylons and any other obstacles.

'Right, I want you to be just here at 1,500 ft,' said Jane, tapping the photograph a mile to the north of the airfield buildings. 'That's on the upwind side. Then just come on down, and you shouldn't really be beyond this fence at 500 ft. If you do end up there, the chances are that you're going to land short of the target.' She glanced at a windsock. 'The wind's going to be about 10–15 mph when you land.'

We were aiming to touch down in the area of a large white arrow; but like the tube map in a London Underground station, it was the only point on the photograph you couldn't find. Hundreds of other tapping fingers had worn it away.

'Any questions on that?'

There were none.

'Fine. If you're in any doubt, have a look down at our canopies below you and see which way we land, and do the same. Just make sure you're heading into the wind for landing and if you come down anywhere on the drop zone, that's fine.'

'Right,' she said, turning to a man in a dark blue jumpsuit, 'this is Rod Bartholomew, who's going to be your Secondary Instructor.'

I shook hands with a tall thin skydiver, his tanned face broken by a smiling brown moustache. Rod and his brother Steve, both AFF instructors, had made the first Tandem jump in Britain only the year before. Between them my two instructors now had more than 4,500 jumps behind them. Together, we went round to the mock-up fuselage for a few last minute dirt dives and then we were walking out to the aircraft.

For some jumpers, the time in the plane is the most nerve-wracking part of the jump; and it's not unusual for people to combine their first jump with their first flight. In those last 25 minutes, as the aircraft climbs to the jump altitude, you're still trying very had to imagine what it's going to feel like when you heave your delicate little body into two and a half miles of airspace.

It isn't easy; nothing you've ever done has prepared you for it. Videos have shown what it looks like. People have told you what it feels like. But it isn't until you walk out to the plane that imagination takes a seat on the grass, and reality grabs you rudely by the scruff of the neck.

Before climbing into the aircraft, there was time for

A final dirt dive in the wind blast behind the aircraft's port propeller. Men should arrange themselves carefully, or the moment of deployment will be an eye-watering experience.

one final dirt dive, standing behind the port wing. With a flatulent splutter, the props of the Islander stuttered and then became a blur. And there, flanked by Rod and Jane in a wind filled with the smell of spent aviation fuel, I rehearsed my lines over the thrumming of the engines:

'Ground, altimeter, shout "x,000 ft" to Rod.'

'Okay!'

'Turn head, shout "x,000 ft" to Jane.'

'Okay!'

'Look, Reach, Pull.

'Look, Reach, Pull.

'Look, Reach, Pull.

'Ground, altimeter, shout "x,000 ft" to Rod.

'Turn head, shout "x,000 ft" to Jane.

'Free Time [waggle tongue vigorously].

'Arm shake at 5,000 ft.

'Ground, altimeter, Shout 5,000 ft to Primary (Jane).

'Pull Signal from Jane . . .

'Look, Reach, Pull.

'1,000, 2,000, 3,000, 4,000 . . . check canopy.'

We were now fully kitted up, but tightening our legs straps – which go round your upper thighs – had been left until we were in the aircraft. Men in particular, are advised to make sure everything is firmly in place; the jerk that you receive when the main canopy opens can otherwise be an eye-watering experience.

We were bundled into the aircraft and slid along inside the narrow fuselage, first Steve, then me. Facing back down the plane I had an uninterrupted view of someone else's back and a pair of goggles.

The most unnerving thing was that for some reason, I *still* wasn't feeling nervous. 'It's definitely good to be nervous,' Jane had said. 'I still get very nervous sometimes. But the day I don't have any nerves at all will be the day I stop jumping. It isn't healthy being totally cool all of the time.'

I wasn't feeling particularly cool or even cocksure; but I was still regarding the prospect of leaving the aircraft with undiluted relish.

The engines stopped puttering and started whining instead; and the port landing wheel, which I could see through the open door, was soon bouncing through the daisies. There were all sorts of things which *should* have been going through my mind; the sequence of my imminent descent – over twice the height of Ben Nevis in 50 seconds – might not have been a bad place to start. Instead, as the nose lifted and the picture of the Kent countryside in the doorway tilted through 45 degrees, I had a series of disconnected thoughts: in the distance the barley had been heavily beaten down by the strong winds; below us, a school bus, a yellow and black dot, was turning a corner into the village of Headcorn; and under my chin, the hand on my altimeter, wound by an invisible finger, was beginning to creep around the dial.

At 1,500 feet, the fibre-glass door was slid into place. And with that, my spectacles, which had already been steaming up around the edges, began to mist over completely. At 3,500 ft the door was opened again, and someone – a girl wearing a shiny blue jumpsuit and an ear to ear grin – very simply and without even saying goodbye, vanished out the door.

Jane was tapping my shoulder. 'What'll you be doing at this altitude?'

We were already at 5,000 ft, twice the height at which static line students make their first jump.

'You'll be tugging my arms to remind me we're at five grand.'

She nodded. 'Good.'

Five minutes later, at 7,500 ft, the door was pulled back again and cold air filled the fuselage. A figure in a black helmet, complete with Biggles goggles, moved to the hole in the fuselage wall and suddenly, he too was gone. By craning my neck, I could probably have watched him for ten or 12 seconds. But like a motorist passing the scene of an motorway pile up, I was trying not to look, rather in the hope that it wouldn't happen to me.

Again the door was eased into place. Steve, now sitting behind me with Jack and H, his two instructors, was staring silently ahead.

At 9,000 ft Jane knelt up in front of me. 'Just lean forward and let me check you over.'

Handles and toggles, AAD, Stephens Lanyard, belly band, altimeter. And finally, under the flap on the back of the rig, The Pin. I suddenly felt like a human hand grenade.

We climbed steadily upwards, through patches of cloud, until sunlight began to brighten the inside of the fuselage. There was a shout from somewhere at the front of the plane.

'We've been cleared to 12,000.'

I wasn't smiling very much but nor was Steve. In front of me, the shiny floor of fuselage, polished by the seats of hundreds of jump suits and so recently vacated by the Smiling Girl and the Man in Black, was now devastatingly empty. I was forgetting to breathe. Rod lent over.

'Big deep breaths. In through the nose, hold it for a second. Then out through the mouth.'

The hand on my altimeter didn't bother stopping at 12,000 ft, but began another circuit of the dial. Again, a voice from the front.

'Okay!'

The plane levelled out. And then, just when my stomach and chest had started to register the first ripplies of nerves, someone farted. I can't pretend that it made me want to leave the aircraft any sooner, but it certainly helped. Rod and Jane reached for the door at the same time; and more than anything, it felt as though the lid had been lifted on a vast bottomless deep freeze. Once more, cold blustery air raced into the interior of the plane, like freezing fingers clawing up my legs and arms. Below us, and framed in the doorway, were fragments of countryside, patched together by white cloudy cement. And there, absurdly, was the motionless black landing wheel. I had the same sense of being magnetised towards the drop that you get if you stand near the edge of a tall cliff on a windy day.

'Okay, Miles. Let's go.'

Hands were put onto four of my seven handles, and I crabbed my way down the plane so that I was sitting, across the fuselage with straight legs facing the gap on the left side of the plane. I tried to focus somewhere between the door and the horizon. But in reality, I wasn't even remotely aware of the ground, only the feeling of nothingness.

Rod tightened his grip on my left leg handle, and the brown hedgerow of a moustache came towards me and shouted the $64,000 question:

'*Are you ready to skydive?*'

It didn't occur to me, even for an instant, to say no. But without seeking the approval of the brain, my voice said, '*Ready!*'

'*Then put your legs out after me.*'

In the next four seconds, I felt a sickening blend of fear and exhilaration. Hands were still holding onto me, I was sliding forward into the slipstream, and turning to face along the aircraft heading. Half of me was now sitting on a small aircraft flying at 70 mph; and the other half was sitting on thin air. Together, brain and bum were struggling desperately to work out how I could possibly have come to be in this ridiculous position. It was like plucking up the courage to jump into a very cold swimming pool. For just a second I felt hollow and watery inside; the feeling I used to have when the Headmaster called me into his office.

With my left leg dangling away in space, I looked in at Jane's face three inches from mine.

'*Check in!*'

'*Okay!*'

And out at Rod,

'*Check out!*'

'*Okay!*'

'*Up, down . . . aaaaaaaaaaaaarch!*'

I pushed away at 12,500 ft, and together we fell, out and down, turning left, down and down and down. Breathing and memory stop dead. All six senses are stunned. For a split second, every cell in your body from your brain to the balls of your feet, is utterly baffled. It's the most sudden and total change in circumstances that you've ever invited them to grasp. And gradually, over the next second or two, they recover from the shock.

It wasn't a fight for stability – the movement was smooth and controlled. But still there was the feeling of brilliant white, eternal emptiness. At first I was falling on my left side, with Rod below me, and Jane above me. Instinctively, your reaction is to right yourself, like a cat turning feet-first from a fall. But somehow, miraculously, fighting its way against all the millions and millions of nervous messages that are screaming around your body, is a single, urgent, communication—'*ARCH!*'

In a moment, when the realisation that you're still alive begins to fade, you find yourself in the same position as the frog in mid-leap. Followed by the most reassuring discovery of all: that there are other highly-experienced frogs on either side of you.

Together, these impressions last perhaps seven or eight seconds, by which time you've fallen roughly the height of the Eiffel Tower. I can remember how it felt now, when I think about it; the memory of it comes back in bits and pieces. But at the time, those first few seconds are like a blinding flash of light.

It's interesting how the brain reacts to what is being delivered to it through your goggled eyes. Normally, you respond to a new experience on the basis of everything else you've done before. But to your poor, defeated brain it seems beyond belief that what you're looking at could, in all seriousness, be solid brown earth and grass, churches, houses, village shops and Chinese restaurants. Surely it must be a huge video screen? Or a fairground simulator?

Ten seconds or so into the dive, I began the first Circle of Awareness.

'*Ground, Alti . . .*'

I *looked* in the direction of the ground, but I wasn't seeing it; then at my altimeter and then under my left arm at Rod, whose grinning face was fluttering in the wind-blast. '*. . . 11,000 ft!*'

'*Okaayeeeee!*'

Then at Jane. '*11,000 ft!*'

'*Okay!*' and a Thumbs Up.

'*Look, Reach, Pull*' I wobbled slightly in the wind-blast.

'*Look, Reach, Pull*'

'*Look, Reach, Pull*'

Another Circle of Awareness.

This was the moment, in training, when I'd been cheerfully calling out '*Free Time!*', rather in the expectation that there'd be time to get the kettle on and have a cup of tea. But now, by the time I'd finished chanting altitudes to Rod and Jane at 7,000 ft, there was perhaps only 10 seconds left before the pull. There was a strange gurgling sound from either side of me and I looked across to see Jane pulling horrible faces and yelling like a football hooligan. Rod was doing the same. And never one to miss a party, I joined them in a short, blood-curdling scream. Three seconds passed, and then they were tugging on my arms. Again, I looked blindly at the ground, focused on the altimeter and turned my head to Jane.

'*5,000 ft!*'

Her right fist and index finger came in and pointed directly at my main handle. Until that point I'd had a horrible feeling that finding that ripcord handle would be like searching for car keys in the bottom of a shopping bag. But happily, my hand landed flat and found it first time; I grabbed it and pulled. The handle and wire ripcord came out in my hand and the wind-blast took my arms back into the stable position.

'If you can hear me, open and close your legs.' Equipped with telemeter and radio, Andy Ring guides another student through the subtleties of canopy control.

'One thousand, two thousand, three thousand, four . . . *Whoooooooooaaaaaaa!*'

The deceleration into total silence was over in an instant. It was though a huge hook had reached down and grabbed me by the scruff of the neck. In that split second, as I felt the first tugs of deployment on my back, two shrinking human dots, to left and right of me, fell away below my feet, blooming a few seconds later into blue nylon canopies. Kent swung crazily and two legs, which I soon identified as my own, jack-knifed up to waist height.

It was more a release than a relief. It was so quiet that I almost expected to hear the Hamlet Cigar piano music tinkling out of the clouds. Instead the only sound was a muted chattering high overhead where the forward edge of the canopy was trembling in the wind. It took about eight or nine seconds to 'get my chute together', rip the steering toggles off their Velcro fasteners and draw them down to knee level, releasing the brakes and taking control of the canopy. A moment later my ears popped.

I was just picking up my bearings when I heard a thin electric voice speaking to me from my stomach.

'Miles. If you can hear me, open and close your legs.'

It was the unmistakably impassive voice of Andy Ring, a mile below my size 11 training shoes. I scissored my legs a few times and Andy again pressed his black beard to the radio.

'That's fine, Miles. You're doing lovely.'

The canopy was very forgiving but I still spent the first few minutes easing gingerly into a series of 270 degree turns.

Two miles or so above me, at the very moment my canopy was filling with fresh Kent air, Steve was also getting his 'knees in the breeze' for the first time.

'I was very nervous on the way up to the jump altitude,' he admitted afterwards. 'Simply because it was the first jump – we had so much to think about. And you're also completely over-awed by the whole thing. You aren't even doing things really thoroughly. I was just thinking, "Remember the sequence of the dive, remember the sequence." I said to myself, "Answer the instructor, get in the door, do the checks."'

How had he felt when he'd moved towards the door for the first time?

'Well I got in the doorway, and I suppose in the back of my mind I was thinking, "Well Christ, this is it. I'm diving out of a plane now." But you don't have the time to think about it. When I'd got into that doorway it was just a conscious process of thinking, "What next?"

'I actually found it quite difficult to shout anything. I was trying to say, "11,000 ft". But it didn't sound like that. It's such an overwhelming experience that it's difficult to remember any little bits of it. It melts into one. It just happened and it was brilliant.'

By now, I was preparing for my final 'run in' to land. Jane and Rod – tiny figures – were standing beside the blue mushrooms of their canopies. It still felt as though I'd sprouted a pair of wings – probably the closest I'll ever come to being an angel. Even now, at 200 ft, as I curved into the final upwind leg and raised the steering toggles into full drive, the ground didn't look in the least menacing. It was only in the last 30 ft that the ground rush began; I picked a point about 40 ft in front of me and a few feet from the arrow. With 20 ft to go, Andy's voice returned,

'Okay, Miles . . . ready . . . *flare!*'

Like a puppet taking control of its strings, I drew the toggles down to knee level and miraculously, the canopy half-glided and half-floated me to a standstill. At least, it would have done, if my feet hadn't been slightly too far forward. The touch-down was even gentler than stepping off a kitchen stool, but my feet went on and my bum and Kent made contact, bringing me to a very full stop.

'*Alright!*,' shouted Jane, running over. 'Welcome to skydiving.'

A kiss caught me full on the north and south.

'How was it?'

'I just can't describe it.'

She laughed. 'Well it went fine. Well done. And well done, Rod too.'

'Well done, Rod?' I said.

Rod was wearing a smile like an estuary.

'Well, yes,' said Jane. 'I told you Rod was an instructor, but he was only awarded his AFF rating yesterday. You were his first real student.'

Half an hour later, we were back in the tiny Slipstream office.

'Okay,' said Jane, 'What I want you to do is tell me what happened from the moment that Rod asked you whether you were ready to skydive.'

In five minutes, I'd told them all that I could remember. And then they began asking questions: had I had any problems reading my altimeter? Had they given me any other signals? And gradually, every last detail came back.

'I think you gave me a signal to straighten my legs, didn't you?'

Jane smiled. '*I'm* asking *you*.'

'Okay,' she said, when I'd dried up. 'That's good recall – you remembered almost everything. I thought it was a pretty good jump. Certainly we weren't having any problems with you at all. A couple of points we need to sort out on your body position, but that'll come.

'Your Hotel Check was good – a nice "Check In" and "Check Out". A good exit from the aircraft but you were a bit de-arched as you left the plane – in other words, your body position was rather flat. It was a couple of seconds before you started pushing your hips forward to arch your spine. You should try to get into that more quickly; but no problem.

'Then you spent a few seconds thinking, "*Whoa!* What's going on here?" And at that point, Rod did actually signal you to do the first Circle of Awareness. But that's fine; I'd told you not to rush and you were just collecting your thoughts.

'So, you went, "Ground, Altimeter . . .' And on the first Circle, you called out at around 11,000 ft; somewhere around there. You looked across at me, and I gave you a clenched fist – the Knees Up signal – because at that point you'd let your knees drop a bit; followed by an Arch signal – a flat open palm – and you seemed to respond, and that was fine.

'Then, you collected your thoughts again and thought, "Practice Pulls". Now from my side – and Rod will tell you about his side in a moment – but from my side, they were excellent. Your right hand went flat onto the main handle every time. I didn't have to help you at all; no problems there. Your second Circle came at about 8,000 ft and you looked across, reported left to Rod and right to me. Again, I gave you the signal to Arch, and at that point I thought you'd established a pretty good flying position.

'Then we went into the Free Time and you were sitting there dreaming a bit, thinking, "Oh No. This is it!" But you must have heard the two of us yahooing and realised that everything was all right, because you started moving your head around and became a lot more aware.

'Then we shook you at 5,000 ft. And immediately you went into your final check. "Ground, Altimeter . . . 5,000 ft" to me. I gave you the Pull Signal. You hesitated for a second or two and then went in for the pull. And again, from my side, the pull was spot on. No problems with that at all.

'The rest of the jump – and obviously, I wasn't there with you all the way – your canopy control looked good; Andy Ring, who was talking to you from the ground, couldn't see you at first because you were behind cloud, but then he thought that maybe you were steering a bit far off the drop zone. Anyway, you lined yourself up beautifully for the run in, and when you got down to 15 ft or so, your flare was good as well. If you'd just kept your feet straight below you, you'd have had a stand-up landing, instead of that little short skid onto your bum.'

Now it was Rod's turn; his first de-brief as a fully qualified instructor. And still more detail about the jump came out, in his short Surrey sentences.

'You was aware. You knew what was going on. Got out into the arch position. Flying really nice. I was really happy. Obviously you was also happy at the time. You was flying straight "down the tube". Your body position was good. And from my side, the Practice Pulls were spot on, just right. Then your knees dropped slightly as we went into Free Time; and you didn't look at me. I was a bit disappointed actually – I thought you might at least have stuck your tongue out or something.

'Anyway, all well. Regrip at 5,000 ft. No problems. You came in for the pull. There I was, watching the deployment. And as the chute started to lift off your back, I let go of you.

'Just one point on leaving the aircraft,' he added. 'It's not so much an exit from the aircraft as an entry into the slipstream. You've got to position yourself in the air. You're trying to present your body correctly to the slipstream. But we'll practise that on the ground; otherwise it was fine.'

What concerned *me* was that I hadn't really taken in that I'd been looking down at solid earth. Or more importantly, the consequences of hitting it.

'Well that's all right,' said Jane. 'After all, it's two and a half miles away when you leave the aircraft. It's really an awareness of your altitude that you're after; and on that dive, you were reading your altimeter perfectly.'

I smiled. 'There'll certainly be plenty to think about next time.'

Rod laughed, 'Did you hear what you just said?'

I shook my head.

'*Next time*.'

And that was that. I was *Cleared to Level II*.

Jane wasted no time in preparing me for my second jump. 'It won't be a lot different from Level I,' she said. 'We'll be leaving the aircraft in the same way – a first Circle of Awareness and two Practice Pulls. And then we'll get you do a couple of Heel Clicks: we'll run through them with you and show you a video in a minute. After the Heel Clicks, you do another Circle of Awareness. Now, if there's still time after that – and by time, I mean if we're above 6,000 ft – I want you to try moving forwards across the sky. More about that in a minute.'

Below 6,000 feet, I would have to keep a constant check on my altimeter.

'On your first dive,' said Jane, 'the altitude awareness came from us; this time, I want you to shout to me when we go through 5,000 ft. Having done that, you should go straight back to looking at your altimeter. And at 4,200 ft, you're going to go in for the pull. So you're actually pulling at 4,000 ft, but without waiting for a Pull Signal from me.'

Rod was explaining Forward Movement. 'Now, there are lots of ways to move around in the sky,' he said. 'In fact, that's the easiest thing to do. The difficult thing is staying still and falling straight down the tube. So what we've got to do is control that movement.

'Let's assume you're in the stable position. Now, to move forward in the sky, all you do is just point your toes a little bit and straighten your legs right out. So you're presenting more resistance to the airflow at the bottom half of your body. You'll begin to move forward across the sky – and also the ground. You actually start to go a little bit head-down. But don't let that upset you; your arms and hands are still spread as they are in the stable position, and it's only your legs that are moving. Your hands stay in much the same place, perhaps coming back just a touch.

'If all's going well, Jane and I should fall back out of your sight at that stage, because you'll be towing us gently across the sky; and then, after a few seconds, you just ease back into the stable position.

'The Heel Clicks involve simply closing your legs, like a pair of scissors so that one heel touches the other. They're designed to make you aware of the rest of your body.

'And that's all there is to it.'

For the moment the clouds were far too low for AFF, and by 1500, with the wind at well over ten knots, even the static line students were firmly grounded. An hour later, the rain came on, punctuated by thunder and lightning. Now and again, throughout the afternoon, eyes could be seen peering upwards through the steamy, rain-streaked windows of the canteen.

At around 1830, Jane appeared through the cigarette smoke.

'Right, Miles and Steve, get your kit on, there's a large hole in the clouds a mile or so the northwest of the drop zone. It's moving this way.'

After hours of waiting and silently wandering around, thinking ourselves into the next dive, it came as a rush. In two minutes, we had all our kit on, just in time to hear a voice over loudspeakers.

'False Alarm. Sorry, it's moving too fast.'

Three more times, it seemed likely that we'd get up; and each time we climbed into our equipment; only to take it all off again. It wasn't until 1930, that the clouds finally dissolved.

As soon as there was 8,000 ft of sky over the drop zone, Jack and H took Steve up for his Level II. Forty minutes later, when he'd landed and carried his canopy back to the packing sheds, Steve was not looking a happy man. Most of the dive had been fine, but when it had come to the pull, he was faced with something that normally only happens in nightmares – he hadn't been able to find his ripcord handle.

As they walked back from the landing area, Jack had a hand on Steve's shoulder.

'Don't worry about it, buddy. You did a whole bunch of other good stuff up there. There was just one

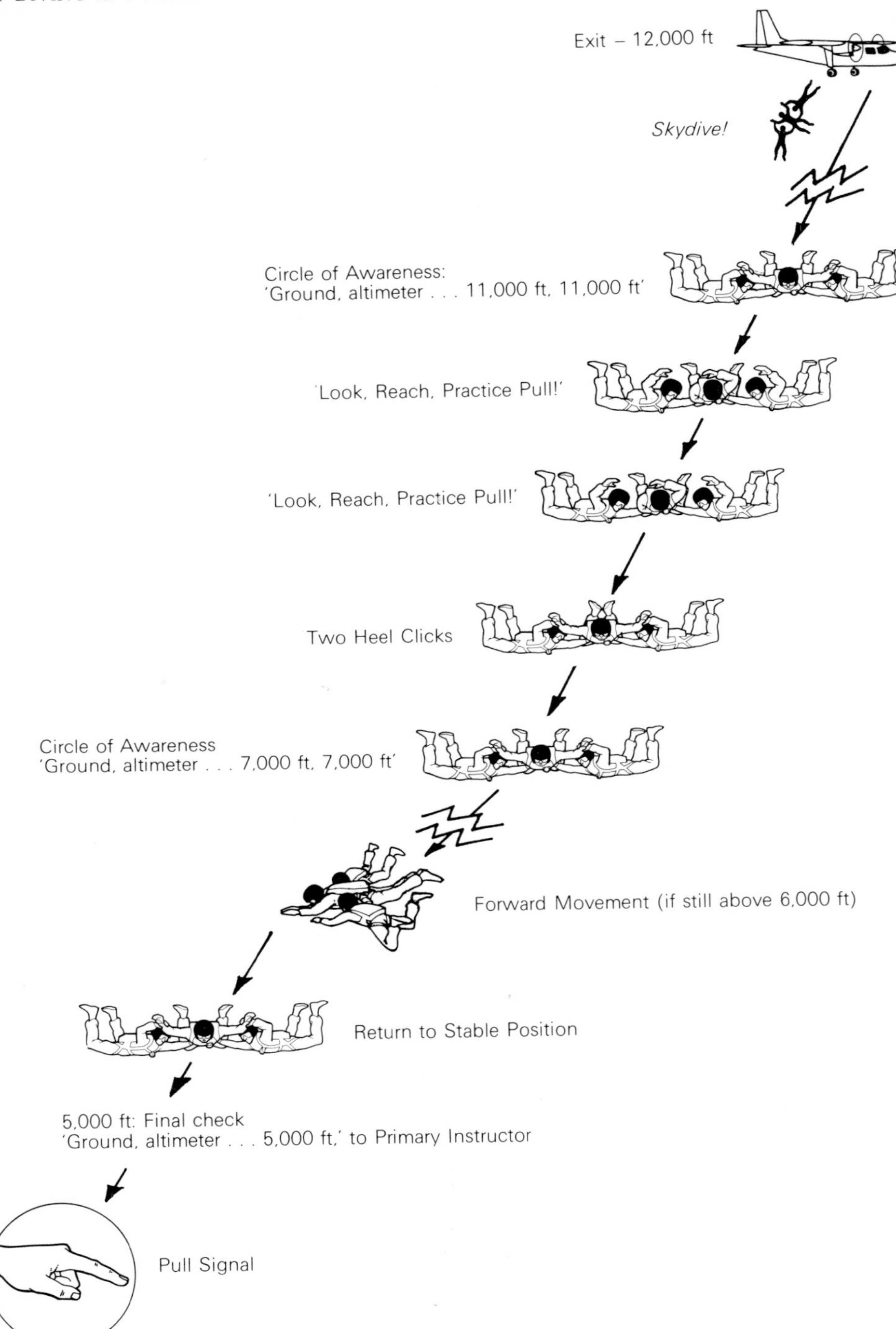
Exit – 12,000 ft
Skydive!
Circle of Awareness:
'Ground, altimeter . . . 11,000 ft, 11,000 ft'
'Look, Reach, Practice Pull!'
'Look, Reach, Practice Pull!'
Two Heel Clicks
Circle of Awareness
'Ground, altimeter . . . 7,000 ft, 7,000 ft'
Forward Movement (if still above 6,000 ft)
Return to Stable Position
5,000 ft: Final check
'Ground, altimeter . . . 5,000 ft,' to Primary Instructor
Pull Signal
'Look, Reach, Pull!
1,000, 2,000, 3,000, 4,000 . . . check canopy!'

Level 2

thing you couldn't find. Don't worry about it. No one's running around, jumping up and down.'

Eventually, Steve smiled. 'It wasn't that bad,' he said. 'We jumped out and everything went perfectly, until I tried to do a 90 degree right turn.

'I started off, and as I looked down towards my right hand, I could feel myself beginning to turn, horizontally, through 90 degrees – beautiful. Then I checked the altimeter, before trying some Forward Movement; I straightened my legs and brought my hands back a touch. Now, I couldn't see the ground at that stage, because there was a bloody great cloud in the way, which we flew down through. And a second or two after coming out of that, we reached five grand, so there wasn't time for anything else. At just over 4,000 ft, I went, "Look, Reach . . . where's the effing handle." I was looking desperately for the main handle and suddenly a hand shot across and grabbed it.

'I'm really annoyed with myself', he said. 'It'll mean that I'll have to do it again. That's expensive. And it's the kind of expense I don't want to have to think about.'

A rejump of Level II would be another £220 ($375).

'I'm sure you'll crack it next time,' I said.

'Oh, I'll crack it,' he said confidently, 'but it just might be more expensive than I'd calculated and I'm not made of money.'

The opening in the clouds had been a brief and expensive one. But it was getting dark now and in the 11 hours since I'd arrived at the airfield that morning, I'd done one jump; been debriefed and 'prepped' for my second one; climbed in and out of a jump suit and rig four times; and mimed my way through several hundred cut-away drills.

It was a fireball sunset. A thick covering of slate grey clouds began to form above the airfield, leaving a narrow band of orange light along the horizon. At 2045, when all the surrounding fields had filled to the hedgetops with white mist, we called it a day. The landscape would have made a stunning sight from 12,000 ft, but jumping into ground mist is as dangerous as jumping into crops: when you don't know where the ground is, it's very easy to flare a little too high, dropping you down very hard.

One jump in two days. Not unusual, but frustrating all the same. We'd have to get a few jumps in tomorrow, before the forecaster's 'ugly weather' came in from Scandinavia on Thursday.

☐ An equal opportunity sport
☐ Level 2: the gut twister
☐ The widening 'bubble of awareness.' Preparing for Level 3 and release?
☐ Heel clicks and disappointment
☐ In search of the stable position
☐ Slow is Smooth and Smooth is Fast
☐ Waiting for sky

DAY THREE

It's a long day. When the weather's bad, the waiting begins at 0845; and if it's good, the last aircraft lift is going up as the sun is going down. At dawn on this Wednesday morning the sky had looked promising, but by nine, white cauliflowers of cumulus were already sprouting around the horizon.

A few lucky people in the world can honestly say of their job: 'There's nothing I'd rather be doing.' Jane Buckle is one of them; and it's probably this, as much as natural talent, that has allowed her to excel at her chosen sport.

Like so many other skydivers, she'd seen a parachuting demonstration at a county show and thought she'd like to have a go. With a friend, she put her name down for a Static Line course and together they did their first jump. Until then, her mother had said she was spending too much time in the house. And as Jane remembers, 'It wasn't long before she was saying the opposite.

'I scared myself silly for 50 jumps or so,' she admits. 'But I liked the atmosphere, I liked the people. I liked the sense of achievement. Above all, I liked the slight element of what I thought at the time was danger. Obviously, I soon realised just how safe it was, but I just got a thrill out of it.'

Before long, someone had encouraged her to compete in novice events at national level. Through a combination of a job that bored her and the prospect of warm clear skies, she was lured to what has become the world's most famous drop zone: Zephyr Hills – Zee Hills for short – near Tampa, Florida. After two months, she'd logged another 80 jumps, all from above 13,000 ft, effectively doubling her 'Time in Freefall' to around three hours.

'The whole learning atmosphere in America is very different,' she says. 'It's very positive, very confident. It's more a question of "You *can* do this." You don't say, "I *can't*", you say, "I'll *try*."

'I couldn't believe how much it accelerated my learning. I went out there as a very basic jumper and came back with a great deal more experience.'

That was in 1981, four years before AFF was brought to the UK. What were her most enduring impressions of the sport after 3,070 jumps?

'Well, obviously, certain jumps are very special. My first jump with ten people at night was amazing. And being tipped out of an upside-down Tiger Moth biplane. But the best thing is the people; I know that I can walk onto any drop zone in the country and be sure to know someone there. Skydiving is a very small world.'

A small world with very different sorts of people. 'You get some very macho types in this sport,' she said, 'especially on the Static Line course. They'll come along thinking they're the first person ever to do it and that they're really wonderful. Sometimes you'll get one of them in the aircraft with maybe seven other blokes in there; and then he'll suddenly realise it's a woman instructor and *zziiiippp!* – he won't say another word.

'Most people have no trouble, but it's always the ones who talk the loudest who'll freeze in the door and have to be encouraged to leave the aircraft. Most people are fine.'

The euphemism is 'encouraging them to leave' but no one is ever forced to leave an aircraft. The most you're ever likely to receive is an firm and encouraging' hand on your shoulder at the moment you imagine your life is about to start to flashing before your eyes. In AFF, probably because of the personal nature of the instruction, 'freezing in the doorway' is virtually unheard of.

Skydiving is certainly not a male preserve. Britain's 30 parachute training centres welcomed 40,000 newcomers – men and women in almost exactly equal numbers – to the sport in 1986.

'Women are certainly very much accepted at Headcorn.' says Jane. And although she wouldn't say so herself, that has much to do with the fact Jane has been working there for six years.

Most students will tell you that the second jump i the one that does the gut-twisting. One departur from the plane has been enough to fill in most of th gaps in your expectations. And now the butterflie start flapping for all they're worth. Fortunately, whe the moment for leaving the aircraft finally arrives, th need to keep reminding yourself of the sequence of th jump seems to be enough to quell most of the nerves

We were standing by the wooden training fuselag and Rod was running through some final points.

'Just remember, you've got a tendency, when yo do your Practice Pulls to forget about arching you spine. If you do that, your position will flatten out an you'll start to cup a bit of air under your chest an stomach. That can raise the front half of your body bit high, so you're no longer horizontal. That won' matter so much on Level II, because we're still holdin onto you. But on Level III, which is the first time w release you, you wouldn't just 'sit up'; you might eve flip upside down. So we've got to get the Stabl Position sorted out now.'

Half an hour later, we were high over Headcorn circling upwards. This time, we only had air traffi clearance to 11,500 ft. When I last looked at m altimeter, the orange hand was touching 11,500 ft and then the sequence began again: the aircraf banked onto the jump run, flying straight into th wind, directly over the top of the airfield.

On the first jump, I'd slid into the doorway wit very little idea what day of the week it was. But now, was much more aware; I knew how weird an wonderful it would feel as we parted company wit the aircraft. Just enough of the 'Wow Factor' ha gone out of it, so that the initial feeling o disorientation wasn't so stunning.

I sat in the doorway, facing into the slipstream wit my legs dangling in space; I took a deep breath of col air and went into the Hotel Check.

'*Check In*.'

'*Okay*,' from Jane.

'*Check Out*.'

'*Okay*,' from Rod.

'*Up, down . . . arch!*'

We fell away. And just as before, I was left shoulde down. We also turned through 90 degrees, but thi time I managed to get stable more quickly. The firs Circle was fine and five seconds later, I went into th two Practice Pulls at 11,000 ft. Twice, my left arn hand curved round above my head, maintaining m symmetry in the airflow as my right hand landed fla on the main handle. Then, through the stream of win and white blotches of clouds, came the heel clicks.

'Hello Feet, this is Brain, are you receiving me?'

On the first one, heel touched ankle. I did it again and training shoe touched training shoe. The third one was straight out of the textbook and I couldn't have felt more elated if I'd suddenly discovered I could fly.

On the second Circle of Awareness, at around 8,000 ft, I had trouble reading the altimeter. The dial is fitted on to your chest band, with the face offset, 90 degrees to the left. This puts 'o ft' in the 9 o'clock position, ensuring that the most important altitudes – from o round to 6,000 ft – are clearly visible; but leaving 8,000 ft and 9,000 ft somewhere under your chin.

By mistake, I looked right to Jane first; then left and right again. Jane's arm and up-turned thumb came fluttering in front of me – the signal for the forward movement: my hands came back very slightly and I straightened my legs. For a moment, I felt perfectly level; and then, quite slowly, I was conscious of being tipped slightly head-down and at the same time, Jane and Rod fell back out of view. There was no sense of moving forwards in relation to the ground. As far as I was concerned, the ground might still have been a hundred miles away. But for the first time, I was suddenly able to focus on the clouds.

On the first jump, I'd only been conscious of anything that was less than three feet from my eyes. It was as if there was a sort of 'bubble of awareness' around me, perhaps only two or three feet wide. I'd seen Rod and Jane but I hadn't felt connected to my feet or lower body. This time, the world was about 25 ft wide. Clouds were no longer simply white blobs – I realised that I was falling towards them. Nor were we falling towards a green and brown canvas of modern art. There was some definition; enough to know that what I was seeing through the blast of cold air was not just abstract brush strokes, but a network of rapidly expanding fields.

After flying forwards across the sky for ten seconds I raised my lower legs and eased back into the stable position at 7,000 ft. Seven seconds later, I shouted 5,000 ft to Jane – a few seconds early at 5,500 ft: thumbs up. From this point on, I'd been taught to keep my eyes on the 'alti' until the pull height at 4,200. But because it was still 4,900 when I looked back at the dial, I allowed myself a brief glance away. Two seconds later at 4,400, I looked back and went in for the pull.

'Look, Reach . . .'

My hand landed on top of someone else's – Jane's. There was just time to think, 'Hang on, this is my job' and then, a second later, we pulled it together. The ripcord came away. And this time, I completed the count before the dangling began.

The time in freefall is over so quickly, that you're tempted to rush through the exercises, to give yourself some more Free Time at the end. But the exercises themselves take every ounce of concentration. You're forced to concentrate more intensely for those 50 seconds than you've ever done before. Until you've stopped swaying, you haven't a clue which way you'll be facing. Orientating yourself after the aircraft has taken off is far from easy. Admittedly, the aircraft's Jump Run over the airfield is almost always into the wind. But the upper winds at 12,000 ft – or 'uppers' as experienced jumpers call them – can often be blowing in exactly the opposite direction to the ground winds. As far as I was concerned, the wind direction was fairly academic: I was still so blitzed by the effects of the wind-blast on the descent and the need to concentrate that I couldn't have picked up my bearings during the fall if the white arrow on the airfield had been a mile long.

I did, however, check the canopy thoroughly. The outermost pockets or cells of the canopy were only partially inflated, but they quickly filled with air when the steering toggles had been released and drawn down.

If a canopy were allowed to fill with air unchecked, the opening would be so violent that the shock would certainly damage the parachute, and may even break the wearer's back. The answer to this problem is the slider – or retardation device. It's a piece of nylon cloth – roughly 18 in. square – which is fitted horizontally in the rigging lines, separating them into four groups where they pass through rivets in its corners. When the deployment sequence begins, the slider is at the top of the rigging lines, immediately below the canopy; and as the canopy fills with air, most of the shock of the opening goes into forcing the slider down the rigging lines until it reaches a fluttering halt, a foot above your head.

After the intense concentration and the battering of the wind, these first few seconds under canopy are like stepping out of a severe gale into a quiet room. Below my feet, there was no movement in the wind socks at either end of the airfield. Andy's electric voice was still chatting away at my waist as I watched the two

Above right Sensory Overload: a student at 12,000 ft on Level 1, just six hours after arriving at Headcorn.

Below right Level 4 exit: the first dive with only one instructor. 'Instinctively, your reaction is to right yourself, like a cat turning feet-first from a fall.'

canopies below me – Rod and Jane – spiralling and tumbling, and then reinflating. This time, I landed on my feet. And as I walked back to the packing sheds, carrying my bundled canopy, the Islander which had carried us to 11,500 ft, swept in, 30 ft overhead and touched down on the airfield beside me.

'Okay,' said Jane, when I'd had a chance to think about it. 'Your Hotel Check was good, the Exit was fine. And when you stabled out, you were in a really good body position. No problems at all. You went straight into your first Circle of Awareness quicker than yesterday, at 11,000 ft or so. Good eye contact with Rod and then me. Then both the Practice Pulls, as far as I was concerned, were good. By that time, though, your stable position had started to flatten out – you weren't arching and you'd let your knees drop again slightly.'

It was at that point, as far as I could remember, that I'd started to feel unstable.

'Well, hang on a minute,' said Jane, smiling. 'What you call 'unstable' and we call 'unstable' are quite different. "Unstable" to us means uncontrolled tumbling. And all you did was rock slightly, which is what we'd call a "buffet". That's not instability; and you're bound to rock just a little bit when you pull. It'll take a lot more jumps before you learn to smooth it out. So honestly, the Practice Pulls were fine.

'I looked back at your legs for the Heel Clicks which were just as you described. Then you pointed your toes upwards and backwards, so you were obviously thinking about your legs, that was good. Then we went into the second Circle. You got a bit muddled and looked over at me first, then at Rod and then back at me again.

'Now when it came to the Forward Movement, you seemed to do it in two halves: your arms came back first and then you thought about your legs. But as soon as you'd straightened your legs right out, you were going across the sky beautifully. Rod and I were being dragged along, just as it should be. Then as you came out of it, the old lower legs came back a bit quickly – and too far. That made you go just a little bit chest-up. And again your knees dropped.

'You looked back at your alti, called out 5,000 ft to me, that was good. But by this time, you'd really started to lose your position. Your knees were coming down and you were in a very flat position.'

At that altitude, the instructors don't like to give any more hand signals. 'It might make you lose your altitude awareness and you're only five seconds away from the pull,' said Jane. 'Then I saw you look away

Opposite Level 5: gradually, the bubble of awareness around you grows until quite suddenly, you realise that what you're looking at through the windblast is a rapidly expanding patchwork of fields, roads, churches and Chinese restaurants.

from your altimeter, and I wasn't quite sure what was going on. So I reached for your main handle. And the other reason was simply because of your body position; I wanted to be ready to "dump you out" if you did suddenly go unstable at pull time. I wanted to have my hand there, just in case.

'And then bang on 4,200, your hand came in for the pull, and that was great.' She smiled again. 'Your hand landed on mine; we had a fight for the handle and I won! But not to worry. I'm perfectly satisfied that you'd have pulled it yourself. The fact that my hand was already there is irrelevant.'

So the only real problem was my stable position.

'The main thing,' said Jane, 'is that you know what you're doing wrong. Other than that, your canopy control was fine; you flared a little bit too high on landing, but no problems there. Basically, it was a good jump. Rod?'

'Yeah,' said Rod, expansively, 'it was just that you started to let your feet come back to your bum. A bit of buffetting, a bit of stiffness and I could see you was a little bit tense; you was thinking, "What's going on 'ere?" Just relax. Let the wind take your arms back. Do you know which direction you was facing?'

I didn't. 'But as I went out of the aircraft, I felt that I turned left and dipped my left shoulder.'

'Well, no,' said Jane, 'it wasn't you. It's just that

A static line student wearing the conventional training rig: a back-mounted main parachute and chest-mounted reserve.

when we do an AFF exit, what happens is that, as Rod leaves the aircraft he's caught by the blast of the slipstream; as I go off a second later, I get my chest in the slipstream. You're actually facing 90 degrees left, with him below you and me above you, which is why you felt you were left-hand-low. That's not your fault – it's just the way the exit happens. All we did was turn 90 degrees left which doesn't matter at all.'

'One other point on canopy control,' said Rod. 'You're never going to be able to steer the parachute in perfect right angle turns as you come down. It's always going to be more of a gradual turn. Every time you're under canopy, the wind's going to be a bit different. You've just got to be smooth under your parachute.

'On landing, if you've got your toggles right up as high as they'll go – in other words, you've released the brakes completely – you're allowing the parachute its full forward gliding potential. Remember, the parachute must be on Full Drive to give you the most effective flare. What the flare is doing is converting all your forward speed into lift at the moment your feet touch the ground. A square parachute behaves very much like an aircraft wing. You *can* flare a parachute from half brakes, but it's not as effective.'

I'd learnt far more than I had on the first jump, and I'd certainly enjoyed it, but at the same time, it had required so much concentration that I still wasn't entirely sure what was going on around me during the fall. In the words of the experts, I wasn't yet 'air aware.'

'Given the choice,' I told Jane, 'I'd really like to do one jump that didn't involve any exercises at all. Nothing but falling, watching the ground, looking around, and taking in the rate of the fall.'

'Well, don't worry,' she said, 'that's basically what you're going to be doing on Level III. We're just going to be concentrating solely on your body position next time. But that awareness comes. You don't have to do an extra jump to develop it.'

This, more than anything else, should give you an idea of the detail and care with which the AFF instructor can train and watch a student. There were now just two jumps in the logbook and my total Time in Freefall had reached 1 minute 45 seconds. Nothing much to shout about, but by the time a student on the Static Line course accumulates that amount of time in freefall, he or she will have completed around 15 jumps.

Level III *was* very basic: a Circle of Awareness; three Heel Clicks and another Circle of Awareness.

Level 3 (First Release Dive)

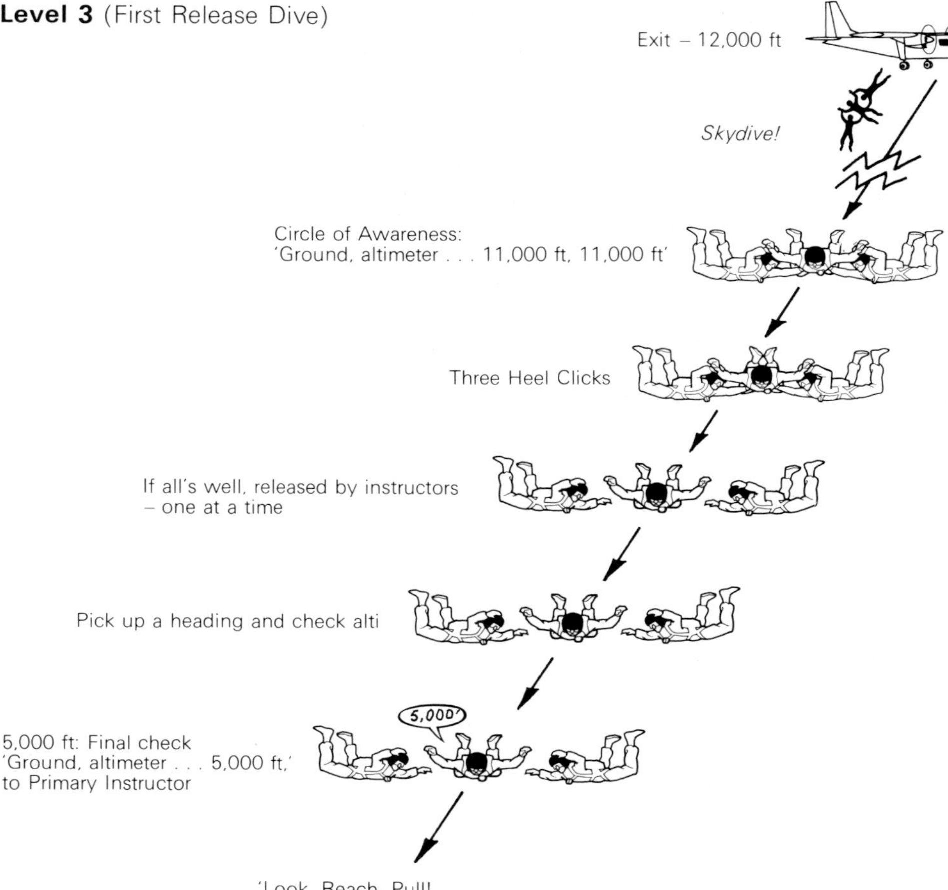

'After that,' said Jane, 'assuming you're flying in a good position, we're going to release you, one at a time. The Secondary will let go first, and if everything's going well, then the Primary. Until that point, we'll probably be holding you very lightly, so you shouldn't even know when we've released you.'

I was assured that they wouldn't just be leaving me there. 'We'll be staying very close to you,' said Rod. 'It's just to give you some time on your own. You've proved that you can fall with the two of us holding onto you and now you've got to do it by yourself.'

From the moment of release, it was business as usual, reporting 5,000 ft to the Primary Instructor. 'If I'm not right at your elbow,' said Jane, 'or if you haven't actually made eye contact with me, you must go back to your altimeter and pull at 4,200 as usual. Don't just spend the next 3,000 ft enjoying the view.'

The main thing, they told me, was not to panic just

because the instructors weren't in their normal place. 'We won't have let you go unless we're quite happy with your position. But if you are tumbling, think very hard about arching – push out your hips. And only then, if you really can't get stable, you'll have to pull – simply because you'll have lost your altitude awareness. That's being very negative, but it's something we have to tell you.

'Finally,' she said, 'we'd like you to think about picking up your bearings and try to identify some feature on the ground. Ideally you should be falling on a constant heading. The jump after this one – Level IV – is all about turning in the sky we can't teach you those until you're learnt to fall on a chosen bearing.'

'That's it,' said Rod. 'It just comes down a good arch.'

I was sent away to think about it; and as it turned out, there was plenty of time. London Air Traffic Control had said that they were very busy and added that it probably wasn't worth making any requests for clearance in the controlled airspace above 5,500 ft for at least another hour. We waited all afternoon. While the wind remained below ten knots, the static line students carried on tumbling out at 2,500 ft. But then they, too, were held up as it started to gust to over 15 knots.

It wasn't until nine hours later, at 2030, that we got a break in the clouds, and a chance for a final lift of the day. The light was beginning to fade and it was much colder. But having thought about it all afternoon, I was still determined to go. Above all, I'd been trying to concentrate on arching, to establish a really strong stable position.

On this lift, I was sitting in a different place in the

In search of the stable position: spread-eagled on a packing table, Jane Buckle, Miles Clark and Rod Batholomew run through the sequence of the dive.

aircraft, no longer beside the door, but well forward and facing the tail, with another eight jumpers crammed in front of me.

The door was covered over again and we continued to 11,000 ft through gossamer clouds. Now, warm yellow sunlight was streaming into the plane, so that the shadows of pilot and parachutists were projected down onto the rear of the fuselage. This watery sunlight above the clouds made the ground seem very grey and remote, almost as though there was no ground there at all.

My harness felt tight and awkward. I wasn't breathing again; and if the truth be known, I wasn't a happy man. The floor space in front of me was empty again and I was moving towards the door. I realised that I'd been feeling much happier about the jump earlier in the day. Everything had come in a rush. I climbed into the doorway and gulped through the Hotel Check.

'Up, down . . . arch!'

We curved away into the slipstream, cold and funereal, at 12,000 ft. But after recovering from the realisation that this, at last, was it, I stabilised and got the first altitude reports out at 11,000 ft. A second later, a fist – the Knees Up signal – appeared in front of me; and I forced my toes upwards and backwards. This, I found, was the easiest way to raise the knees. My heels clicked somewhere behind me, but already my position was flat; I knew I'd lost the position and I wriggled and rocked.

After the second Circle at 9,000 ft, I felt Rod let go, but Jane was holding on stubbornly, like a crab on a piece of meat. She was still right beside me and 2,000 ft (ten seconds) later I felt her release me.

When pull time arrived, I screamed out the count as the canopy burped open overhead and just as before, the direction I was facing was still a complete mystery until the swaying had stopped. I was just glad that it was over.

An hour later, when I'd thought about it for a bit and bought the teas and coffees, we sat down in the 'Headmistress's Office'. I'd felt stiff and robotic; and that seemed to sum up the whole jump. I was trying too hard, concentrating too much on just one thing: forcing my body into an arch.

'Being in a different place in the aircraft can certainly make a difference,' said Rod, 'but you've got to get used to that as you get more experienced.

'Your exit was good, though,' he said. 'You didn't rush. But then, soon after we'd left the aircraft, you immediately started to rock. You gave the first Circle

Please release me: a cold grey evening at 11,000ft.

at 11,000 ft, which was fine, still rocking. But you went ahead and did your Heel Clicks and they were spot on. That was simply because, when you put your legs back for the clicks, they came through the position they should always be in when you're in the stable position; but as soon as you'd done the heel clicks, your feet came straight back to your bum again. We carried on down and you was gettin' signals from both Jane and meself – "*Straighten legs, straighten legs*." – and you tried. I saw your lips move, so I knew you'd understood it. Then you started to rock again, and there was a slight turn to the left through that period, but that's nothing to worry about.

'Then came the second Circle. But when you looked at me, you didn't get a thumbs up – I gave you another Straighten Legs, which you didn't really respond to. Anyway, the dive continued – you was bouncin' around, really stiff, legs tucked right up.'

And then came the revelation.

'We didn't in fact let you go. I just had a gentle grip; I looked over to Jane and she wasn't happy either. So we just held onto you.

'You came in for the pull, a little bit high at around five and a half grand. But then height is all safety. Not a big problem. All right?'

A disappointed smile.

'So, to sum up then: It wasn't a good dive. But it certainly wasn't a horrendous one. It was okay. What is good is that we can sort the problems out. Now, you're going to have a lot of bad dives. Everyone has bad dives. So don't let it get you down, you've got to get up and come back fighting. We've just got to work on your position.'

Jane was climbing back into her suit to go up with another student. 'So it's another Level III,' she said, 'Got to be, I'm afraid. Simply because we didn't let go of you.'

I was disappointed. But I can't say that I'd had to scrape myself off the floor with surprise.

I spent the next half hour lying face down among the wastepaper baskets on the floor of the Slipstream office, with Rod bending my legs and arms into the right position. 'Just relax.'

I relaxed.

'Not too much.'

I tensed up.

'Lift your knees. Come on, lift your knees.'

Bloody agony.

'Chest down and knees up. Knees up, up, up.'

Just to make things more interesting, one of my legs seemed to want to take up a slightly different position from the other. 'Just arch the spine, push out the hips. Best parts forward,' said Rod. 'Look at the ceiling. Point the toes.'

The main thing, he said, was not to make any radical movements. 'Everything should be nice and slow. It's like driving a car,' he said. 'If you're driving at speed and you see a hedgehog in the road, you wouldn't swerve to avoid it or you'd roll over. It's exactly the same with skydiving. Just ease into everything. Just remember: Slow is Smooth and Smooth is Fast.' By the time we'd finished, I was very clear about what I mustn't do, but by now the list of things I did have to think about seemed impossibly long.

As we locked up the office, Rod was determined that I shouldn't feel disappointed. 'Don't worry about it, mate,' he said. 'I don't really like jumping in the evening after a long day. This afternoon, it's been stop . . . start . . . stop . . . start. You don't know whether you're coming or going. It's easy to forget or relax and stop concentrating on the skydive itself.'

It was now nearly nine-thirty.

'I think that has a lot to do with it,' he said. 'And anyway, one skydive is reckoned to be equivalent to a seven hour working day in terms of mental strain: the build up, the jump and then the climbdown.' He rolled his eyes. 'You get in the pub afterwards, and after half a pint you're like a bag of washing.'

I was.

DAY FOUR

- ☐ Thinking yourself into the dive
- ☐ The sensitive question of cost
- ☐ Rejumping Level 3
- ☐ Rockin' and rollin' at 7000 ft
- ☐ More disappointment
- ☐ Steve takes a tumble
- ☐ Skydiving around the world
- ☐ Rejumping Level 3 (again)
- ☐ Success at sunset

I was lying on the bed again, thinking. A slice of white early morning sunlight, swirling with specks of dust, had found a gap between the curtains, and was spotlighting the floor. I'd spent most of the night reliving the last jump. And now, my thinking had become deafening. Nervousness had been replaced entirely by apprehension. To be honest, I wasn't enthralled with the prospect of another dive; but I realised that it was only because I felt I'd failed an exam – and no one enjoys doing retakes.

'In the end,' Rod had said, 'you've just got to sit there with your eyes closed and imagine your way into it. Try to create a series of pictures of the dive in your mind; so when you do it for real, you suddenly think, "Hey, I've been here before. *Déjà vu*. All right!"'

You certainly do need time to think yourself into each dive, but there's a happy balance between too much and too little.

When I reached the airfield, Steve was busy 'prepping' for his Level IV. And he, too, was thinking.

'I find it takes at least a couple of hours to let the sequence of the jump percolate through,' he said. 'I have to get myself calmed down with the idea.'

Jack was determined not to hurry him into the sky. 'You just let me know when you wanna go,' he said, 'and then we'll do it; and anytime you feel you're not ready, just let me know and I'll say, "Hey buddy, this is your skydive." We'll wait all day for you if you want to. I just don't want to rush you out of the plane.'

Steve said, 'I normally just wander around, talking myself through it. I like to be on my own, round the back of the sheds and just go through the motions.'

We were now at slightly different stages on the learning curve. Partly because I was still stuck on Level III, while Steve was about to try his first 360 degree turns; and partly because we were learning the skills of moving around the sky in a slightly different order.

As Pete Gannaw explained, 'AFF has to have a framework – Level 1, Level 2, Level 3 and so on. But real live human beings are a lot more mushy than that. People progress differently, individuals need to be treated individually. So, for some people there'll be a Level 2½ and others, maybe Level 3¼.

We were now half way through the week, the period that Steve and I had allowed for the course, and it was far from certain that we would walk away at the end of it as fully qualified, card-carrying sky-divers.

'My main consideration,' said Steve, 'is still, "Am I going to get it right?" On the first three jumps, it was more a question of "These dives are £220 a piece; I can't afford a rejump." But it's too late for that: I've already had to have one, and from now on till Level VI, it's £100 a time. So now, I just think, "If I have to rejump Level IV, so be it."'

This question of money is a difficult one. The instructors are well aware of the extra pressure that it puts on a student. Partly for this reason and partly as a matter of etiquette, the business of a student's Jump Bill isn't brought up until the end of the course. As Jane explained, 'All instructors are taught that they mustn't – under any circumstances – progress a student, simply because he or she can't afford to do a rejump. You've got to think very carefully. There is a lot of pressure. But I think there's only ever been one student who has managed to go through in the minimum number of jumps.'

Steve was doing this course as a student on a grant and a loan; and when Jack had had to pull his main ripcord for him, it was the first time that he'd started to have doubts about what he was doing.

'Yesterday, I thought, "Why did I start this? I could just mess this up again and again and again. Maybe I'm just wasting time and money here." But that didn't last for long. To get it right, you've got to take your time. On my last jump, I took time, got it right and my confidence just rocketed.'

The attitude to beginners, particularly those who show commitment to the sport, is very refreshing. Far from being seen simply as novices, newcomers are genuinely welcomed to the party.

'They're very much the lifeblood of the sport,' says Jack, 'but it's more than that, particularly in AFF. As an instructor, you have to get to know people and communicate with them. You have to have some idea how they'd react in a given situation.'

As Chris Kuhle, who learnt through the slower conventional course, remembers, 'I didn't get onto freefall until the 20th jump – in other words I had 19 jumps on static line. And every time I walked back to the sheds after a jump, everyone would crowd round and ask, "How did you do?" Everyone takes an interest. They don't ignore you or think, "Oh, he's just a beginner", which can happen in a lot of sports.'

It was already 1215 and I still hadn't had a jump. Still the waiting went on, so I drove into Headcorn for a pork pie.

'No, it's good for my custom,' said John Fitzharris, owner of the village shop, when I asked him about the comings and goings at the airfield. 'But there's a hard core of resentment to anything that's anyway commercial here. They'd have this village dead, certain people.'

And the aircraft noise? He laughed. 'No,' he said, 'a few of 'em don't like the incessant noise, and some people find the old prop planes rather annoying; I don't. It's nostalgic for me – I'd rather have them than screaming jets.'

Headcorn and the neighbouring village of Smarden are the original sleepy English backwaters, the sort that fill the postcard racks, and if I'd been living here, I don't think I'd have been able to raise the energy to complain about anything.

It was another start-stop-start-stop afternoon. As usual, we were waiting for a hole in the sky. Finally, at around 1400, Debbie Fulford pressed the button on the microphone in the Manifest Hut.

'20-minute call for the following people . . . Clark, Buckle, Saberi, Gregory, Beard, Batholomew, Schreve, and Johnson.'

We walked out to the edge of the airfield, and by the time we were clambering into the aircraft, the gap in the clouds was already well over the airfield. Again, the Islander trundled to the end of the airfield, where rabbits were nibbling the grass, quite undisturbed by the hum of the propellers. This time, as we climbed to the jump altitude, I closed my eyes and went through the jump five or six times, all the time thinking, 'Legs, legs, legs.'

We were cleared for 10,000 ft, but at the rate the clouds were moving, the airfield was soon almost obscured. It seemed very likely that this would be nothing more than an aeroplane ride.

Jane had other ideas. 'We're going to do a short run-in and get out over the edge of this blanket of cloud.'

Viewed from another aircraft, it would have made a marvellous sight. A small twin-engine Islander emptying its load of human dots down a funnel in the clouds.

There was only time for a brief flutter of nerves in the doorway and then I thought, 'Let's do it'.

We fell away and this time, the wind-blast felt more like a continuous wave of cold liquid. In a few seconds, I was stable enough to be able to smile at Rod on the first Circle of Awareness at 9,000 ft. In 12 seconds, our rate of fall had created a wind-blast of just over 90 knots – equivalent to one and a half times the force of a hurricane. Everything, my cheeks, jumpsuit, even my eyebrows were chattering in the airflow. Spread apart, my black-gloved hands were rising and falling in front of me. I was much more relaxed, looking down *and* forward this time, not just straight below me. Three heel clicks; and each time, one training shoe connected with the other. I did one more for luck. And then, very suddenly I was aware of the ground for the first time: there were individual buildings and trees. I still hadn't a clue which buildings they were – private houses, farm houses or the Unigate dairy. But I'd seen them, and two seconds later, Rod let go.

I looked down at the ground and in celebration at this new found awareness, my lower legs hinged back again and the rockin' and rollin' began again, just in time for the second Circle of Awareness at 7,000 ft. Through wind-buffeted spectacles, I saw Jane stabbing two gloved fingers in front of me, telling me to straighten my legs, but the message wasn't getting through. Something bashed across my legs and Rod appeared at my left elbow again and took a hold. I checked the alti – 5,200 ft – and gave Jane the 5,000 ft signal.

Look, Reach . . . Pull! 1,000, 2,000, 3,000 . . . Cruuuuuummp! The canopy mushroomed overhead. I grabbed the toggles, took control, cleared my ears and felt disappointed. I knew they hadn't let me go. And I knew what that meant.

Gliding down under 340 sq ft of nylon, I was thinking about what I should have been doing 30 seconds before. I was concentrating so hard that I glided downwind for too long at 30 mph or so over the ground. Too late, I turned into the wind for the final leg, so that at 300 ft I was hanging over the stream, and even on Full Drive with the steering toggles as high as they'd go, the angle between me and the stream wasn't changing. At the last moment, 100 ft or so from the water, the wind held its breath and the canopy carried me forward onto the edge of the DZ.

I knew exactly what had gone wrong; as long as I'd been concentrating on my legs everything was fine. But when I switched my attention to the ground or something else, my heels were flipping down onto my bum like the bar on a mouse trap.

As soon as a minute after landing, you have to search back into your sub-conscious to remember what happened. It's more like trying to remember something that happened a week ago. But again, I talked my way through it.

Jane was sitting with her feet up on the desk. 'Okay,' she said. 'Taking it from the top: we tumbled out the door and you were flying really well. No problems with your position at all. Your first Circle, the clicks and second Circle were fine. And when you'd finished that lot, you'd just started to let your legs come back.

'I looked over at Rod and gave him the nod. And as soon as he'd released you at 6,500 ft, your lower legs came up and we rotated through about 270 degrees.'

I hadn't noticed a thing.

'Well it wasn't violent,' she said, 'But because we turned, Rod was behind us. And with your lower legs right back, I wasn't happy about releasing you. If I'm going to release, I like to do it above 5,000 ft. It wasn't a spin or anything. Just a steady turn. So then Rod came back round into position to your left. Now, he didn't really have to grab you; he just took a finger grip again. Then I gave you a signal to straighten your legs at about 5,500 or 6,000 ft. But you still weren't getting your knees up and you were a bit 'chest up'. So I got hold of your arms to push the upper half of your body down a bit, so that you were flying level.'

Rod's release and the regrip had taken just eight seconds. 'But not to worry,' said Jane, 'your altitude awareness was still very good throughout. And the pull and recovery were excellent. We've *still* just got to get this position sorted out.'

A week or so before the course, I'd arranged for one of Britain's leading skydiving photographers, Simon Ward, to come to Headcorn to do the stills for this book. In the last seven years, he has logged more than

1,600 jumps, most of them with around 10 lbs of cameras bolted to his helmet. When he arrived at Headcorn that afternoon, it was clear that he was even more laid back than his telephone voice had suggested.

'So you wanna be a skygod eh?'

'Yes, Simon. Just like you.'

By luck, we'd agreed on Thursday afternoon for the first picture-taking jump, and Jane asked him if he could 'jump video' as well as a stills cameras. 'It'll give Miles a very good idea of what he's doing with his legs.'

And that meant *another* rejump of Level III.

Meanwhile, Steve had made his first attempt at Level IV – by all accounts, a sobering experience: 'It felt a bit strange because there was no second instructor,' he said. 'It was just Jack and me this time. We went out at a very steep angle, too steep. I was arching away, and slowly, we just rolled over till I was on my back.'

As they went over, Steve caught a glimpse of Jack who was still holding on to him. 'Jack's momentum in the roll took us right round on to our front again. But I'd no idea what was going on. I thought, "I'm doing it right, why isn't it happening? Why aren't I coming level?" But I carried on arching and the next thing I knew Jack was in front of me. A few seconds later, he let me go. At that point, Jack was smiling away and his fingers were only inches from mine. So I went into the right turn, and suddenly, my arms and legs just went.'

In about two seconds, Steve lost his bearings and was spinning head down. 'I don't remember it clearly,' he said. 'I was just tumbling around. We came stable for a second; Jack grabbed my leg and then all of a sudden, we went again, just tumbling down and down. At one point, I saw him just below me, looking up. And I suppose I was just searching for security, but I grabbed him by the arm and the waist and wouldn't let go.'

Jack was trying to break Steve's hold, so that he could regrip him properly. But Steve was hanging on stubbornly like a terrier with it's teeth in a leg of lamb.

'Jack was doing his best to fly us back into the stable position, but we were still tumbling about. And when I saw his face for a second, it was a picture of strain. I can't say I was being much help.'

He shook his head. 'Jack wasn't concerned because *he* was fully aware of the altitude. But I was bleedin' concerned, I can tell you. We just about got stable again; I checked my alti – 4,200 – so I pulled.' And that meant another expensive rejump of Level IV.

Headcorn was enjoying it's best afternoon for weeks and the airfield went back to being T-shirt City. All over the grass between the Manifest Hut and the rows of light aircraft, multi-coloured canopies were spread out in various stages of packing, their owners bent over, tucking, pleating and folding. Here and there, bodies lay against their rigs, eyes closed and chins raised to catch the rays.

Other groups were tumbling out of the silent door of the mock-up, dirt diving in preparation for four-man and five-man formations – some of the skills of 'Relative Work'. Sometimes, as many as eight jumpers would be standing on the grass, bent forward, nose to nose, arms raised frog-style, or pirouetting in a strange kind of primitive tribal dance, turning and regripping, nodding and releasing.

If this was the English summer, it lasted for just two hours. By mid-afternoon, the first huge blobs of rain were staining the concrete beside the packing sheds. And the canteen was doing a roaring trade.

Clearly, other countries are less weather-bound than the United Kingdom. But I wondered whether were was anything different about jumping in other parts of the world. Does the air itself feel any different?

Again, Jane gave up: 'Yes it is different, but it's very hard to describe. You'd have to try it yourself to notice the difference.'

'The air, itself? No,' said Pete Gannaw. 'But then, flying is very much in the mind. It's mental control. And you know, it doesn't matter what part of the world you're in; if your second-last wife turns up to ask for the alimony money, that next dive is going to be a lousy skydive. Or if the mortgage is overdue, it's the same.'

It's more the atmosphere on the drop zone itself that differs. 'At Zee Hills,' says Jane, 'it's just, "We're here to have a good time." But in England it can be very frustrating. I find that some people on English drop zones have a very negative attitude. For instance, I might say, "Right, we're going to do this dive. I want you to take this position in the formation," and they'll say, "But I *can't*", or "All right, I'll have a go but I'll probably mess it up." In America, though, if you say, "I want you there, or over here", they just say, "Fine." If you've been asked to take up a certain position in a formation, you may think, "I don't know if I'm going to be able to do that." But you wouldn't dare tell them that, because you'd try. And more often than not, you'd find that you could.'

In the last ten years, skydiving has risen dramatically in popularity around the world. More than 30 countries sent skydivers to the last World Championships; and among the more recent arrivals on the international skydiving scene was a team from the People's Republic of China.

'They're very young,' said Jane. 'They seem to start training them at about 15 and by the time they're 18, years old, they've got 3,000 jumps. They're very good. The jumpers I've seen jumping Classics [style and accuracy] are very hot on accuracy.'

At 1830, the sky was looking better, and Jack was even more optimistic than usual. 'Looks like we've got some sky coming in here.'

It was chilly now. Overhead was a loose-knit blanket of bubbly cloud with blue sky appearing through it; and away to the northwest, between a slow-moving layer of slate grey stratus and the horizon, the sky was pale pink.

Rod was away for the afternoon, so I had a new Secondary Instructor. Dave Spencer, fair-haired with Californian good-looks, exudes the sort of confidence that you'd expect in a man with over 5,000 jumps in his logbook, some of them from as high as 47,000 ft. The other instructors had always been smiling and relaxed in the aircraft, but Dave seemed able, quite effortlessly, to take nonchalance to new heights. For 25 minutes, as the plane climbed through a cold grey sky, he was chatting to Simon Ward about the latest Bond movie, as casually as if he was travelling on a No. 9 bus.

Through the window at my elbow, I could see the detail of the airfield beginning to fade. The landscape was washed in a faint amber glow, but this time, there was no strong sunlight to brighten the interior of the plane. It got steadily colder and darker. Just as we reached 3,000 ft, clearance came through for 'nine grand'.

At 'three-five', someone disappeared out the door, followed a few seconds later by two more figures – a man and woman in floral jump suits, gripping each other's shoulders as they fell out the door with a 'Ready, Set, *GOOoooooo*!'

When it comes to inviting AFF students to leave an aircraft, Dave Spencer is refreshingly forthright.

'He was in the Army,' said Jane, 'so he doesn't

Above right 4000 ft . . . Pull! With my legs bent back too far, I'm back-sliding away from Jane, who is tracking after me. The pilot chute, already out of the top of the frame, has drawn the main canopy (still in its bag) out of the container, and the suspension lines are straightening, snapping out of their elastic retaining bands.

Above right (inset) High in the sunlit silence: for a seasoned skydiver, the moment – half a mile above the earth – when the parachute blooms above his head, is not the beginning of the jump, but the end.

Below right The next stage: a faultless AFF student could be joining a skydiving formation (Relative Work) a week after finishing his AFF course.

believe in the breezy American skydiving terminology. He'll probably ask you if you're ready to make a "freefall parachute descent". When it came, it was even more truncated than that—more of a growl than an invitation. It was the sort of voice he'd probably been reserving for prisoners of war. He grabbed my leg strap.

'ARE YOU READY TO GO?'

I gave as good as I got. 'Yeah, all right!'

'*Well shove yer legs out!*' And with that he was hanging out over Kent, and I was in the doorway.

'*Check in*', to Jane.

Her face was four inches away. '*Okay*,' she said, quietly.

'*Check out*,' to Dave.

'*OKAY!*'

I didn't even think about leaving the plane. We just went straight into it, left shoulder down; and over the next few seconds, the cold wind-blast started chattering at our faces. I levelled out straight away. I was dimly aware of a body in front of me – a 120 mph cameraman – and in the semi-darkness, it felt as though the whole sky, not just the four of us, was falling.

Dave jabbed two black-gloved fingers out in front of me. My legs straightened; and then he released me. I checked the ground; the fields were grey. Then the altimeter: 7,000 ft. And suddenly, I was flying by myself.

I didn't think, "I'm free. I've done it". Instead there was just the overwhelming relief that, at last, the position was strong enough and Jane had felt able to let me go. At 5,000 ft I looked round and saw her slightly behind and to the right of me, arching hard to keep pace with my slightly faster rate of fall. Three and a half seconds later, we reached 4,200.

'*Look, Reach, Pull . . . 1,000. . .*'

My upper and lower front teeth crashed together as the canopy opened and I felt a large chip of tooth on the end of my tongue. I wouldn't have minded if it had knocked it out altogether; the sense of achievement was massive. And a few minutes later, clouds of roosting rooks and jackdaws were leaving their trees as I came screaming in to land.

At last, I'd felt that stable position, and just like learning to ride a bike, I was now confident that I could get it right every time. Not that Simon's sense of humour would let me get away with that sort of confidence. 'Stable?' he said. 'I've seen a water melon falling more stable than that.'

It was late, and Jane kept the debriefing short. 'The

Above left Miles Clark, Whuffo turned skydiver.

Below left Ring a ring a roses: five members of the British freefall team in training somewhere over England.

The skydiver's passport

exit was fine and Simon was very close to us. It would have made an excellent video, but sadly, the lenses of both cameras had fogged over in the damp twilight air.

'Anyway, you got two signals from Dave, both to straighten your legs; followed by a Knees Up fist. Dave let you go. And unlike last time, nothing happened; you carried on flying fine. The only thing you did was a 90 degree right turn on the pull.'

And there in the logbook, were the magic words: *Cleared to Level IV*.

DAY FIVE

- ☐ Preparing for Level 4
- ☐ Minus one instructor
- ☐ Moving around the sky
- ☐ Confidence and 'the best Level 4 I've ever seen'
- ☐ Preparing for Level 5
- ☐ Steve goes for a spin
- ☐ Helicopter Annie. Crowds and clouds

In the morning, Kent was like a misty scene from *The Lord of the Rings*. The air was soggy – a fine fog was spilling over the hedgerows and the dew was hanging in glistening beads from the fences around the drop zone. At the airfield, figures dressed in shorts, with towels draped around the necks, were flip-flopping along Skid Row. In front of a green nine-by-nine tent, an army chef was firing up his No 2 burners, cooking breakfast for the Royal Engineers' freefall team.

Entering a sport is like visiting a foreign country for the first time with only a schoolboy understanding of the language. Everything is strange and new, but gradually at first, and then quite suddenly, things which at first struck you as unusual, seem normal and commonplace. Already, after just five days on a drop zone, the extraordinary had begun to seem almost ordinary; the idea of leaving an aircraft and losing all contact with the physical world for almost a minute at a time seemed hardly worth a second thought. Rid of its death-defying image, jumping out of aeroplanes had become a very reasonable, sound-minded pastime.

I had finally stepped over the Whuffo Line.

Jane was sitting in the doorway of the mock-up, going through the sequence of my Level IV jump. 'Right. This time there's no second instructor. From here on, it's just you and me; but there's no reason why that should make any difference to you. Now, on this jump, when you've established a good stable flying position, I want you to tell me the altitude; and then I'm going to move round so that I'm facing you. I may actually climb round you, or I may let you go and fly round in front of you. That'll depend on how stable you are. I might have to give you signals before I let you go.

'The exercise we're going to do is this: a 90 degree turn to the left one way; followed by a 90 degree turn, back again, to the right. Then I want you to do some forward movement towards me, in just the same way that you learnt in Level II.

'So going through it from the beginning: when I've moved round in front of you and I'm happy with your position, first of all I'll simply point at your left shoulder, which is the signal to go into the left turn. I'll follow you round as you start turning, and when you've stopped and checked your altimeter again, I'll give you the signal for the right turn.'

If there was still enough sky below us, she wanted me to repeat the exercise. 'But that would be a bonus – the first part is the important bit. On this jump, the cut off altitude is 6,000 ft: at that height – wherever you are, whatever you're doing – you stop working. I'll make sure that I'm in front of you. At that point, I want you to shake your head, just to let me know that you're not going to do any more exercises. And then just keep watching your altimeter down to 4,000 ft.'

Learning to turn with the aid of Jack's kinky green harness.

'Fine.'

I'd said, 'Fine', but there was now even more to concentrate on. Two 90 degree right turns, *as well as* trying to remember everything else? I'd discovered very early in this course that you don't have the luxury of consolidating on lessons learnt – if you've achieved something once, it follows that you must be able to do it again.

When Jack had arrived on Tuesday, he'd brought a special training harness with him; a rather kinky green thing, in which a student can be suspended horizontally in the stable position a few feet above the ground. Jane strapped me into it, and I swung forward until I was face down, 18 in. above the daisies.

'Okay . . . Left and right turns.' Jane was kneeling beside me.

'Now I just want you to imagine that you're holding a broomstick across your shoulders, with your arms hanging over it, but bent at the elbow, so your hands are out forwards just as they are when you're in the stable position. The imaginary broomstick is just keeping your shoulders exactly level; if you lower one shoulder, the other one comes up, but the rest of the body and legs should stay as they are in the stable position.

'As you alter the angle of your shoulders and arms relative to the ground, what's happening is that, instead of flowing round you evenly, more air is being deflected off to one side of you than the other: that'll put you into a turn. In fact, if you're leaning with your left shoulder down, you'll continue to fall vertically down the tube, but you'll also start to turn to the left. The main thing is that it's only your shoulder and arms that are moving. You're keeping them in a straight line, in the same plane if you like. Just think of your shoulders and arms as an aircraft wing. One side is dipping, the other is rising exactly the same amount, just like the wings when the plane is banking in a turn. At the same time, you should be turning your head to look over the back of your lower hand; in other words, in the direction you want to turn. The main thing is not to be violent. It's just like everything else you've learnt; go into it nice and slowly at first.'

She wasn't looking for precise 90 degree turns. 'All I want to see is control. It's also important that you don't just drop one shoulder and arm and forget about raising the other side. Everything in skydiving is symmetry – either presenting a symmetrical body position to the airflow when you want to fall down the tube and on the same bearing; or modifying it on purpose, in order to move around the sky.'

After I'd spent ten minutes or so in the harness playing aeroplanes, Jane put out a hand and stopped me in mid-turn. 'Right, what I want you to do now, is just go and have a think about that for a little while. And then we'll go through it again, both in the harness and from the wooden mock up. I don't want to rush you into this; there's quite a lot more for you to do on this level.'

Judging by Steve's three attempts at Level IV, there certainly was.

The tannoy was talking again:

'Right, there are lots of people out here waiting to jump. Can we get a few pilots and things together?'

Pilots appeared and two strings of eight static-line students were led out to the aircraft. An hour later, in the middle of the morning, Jane and I were once more on our way out to the plane.

It was 1100 and the sky over Headcorn was huge – there wasn't a cloud in sight. Through the open door of the plane, I could see small coloured dots moving along the dark lines of the roads. In the distance, a

Dirt-diving for Level 4

Level 4

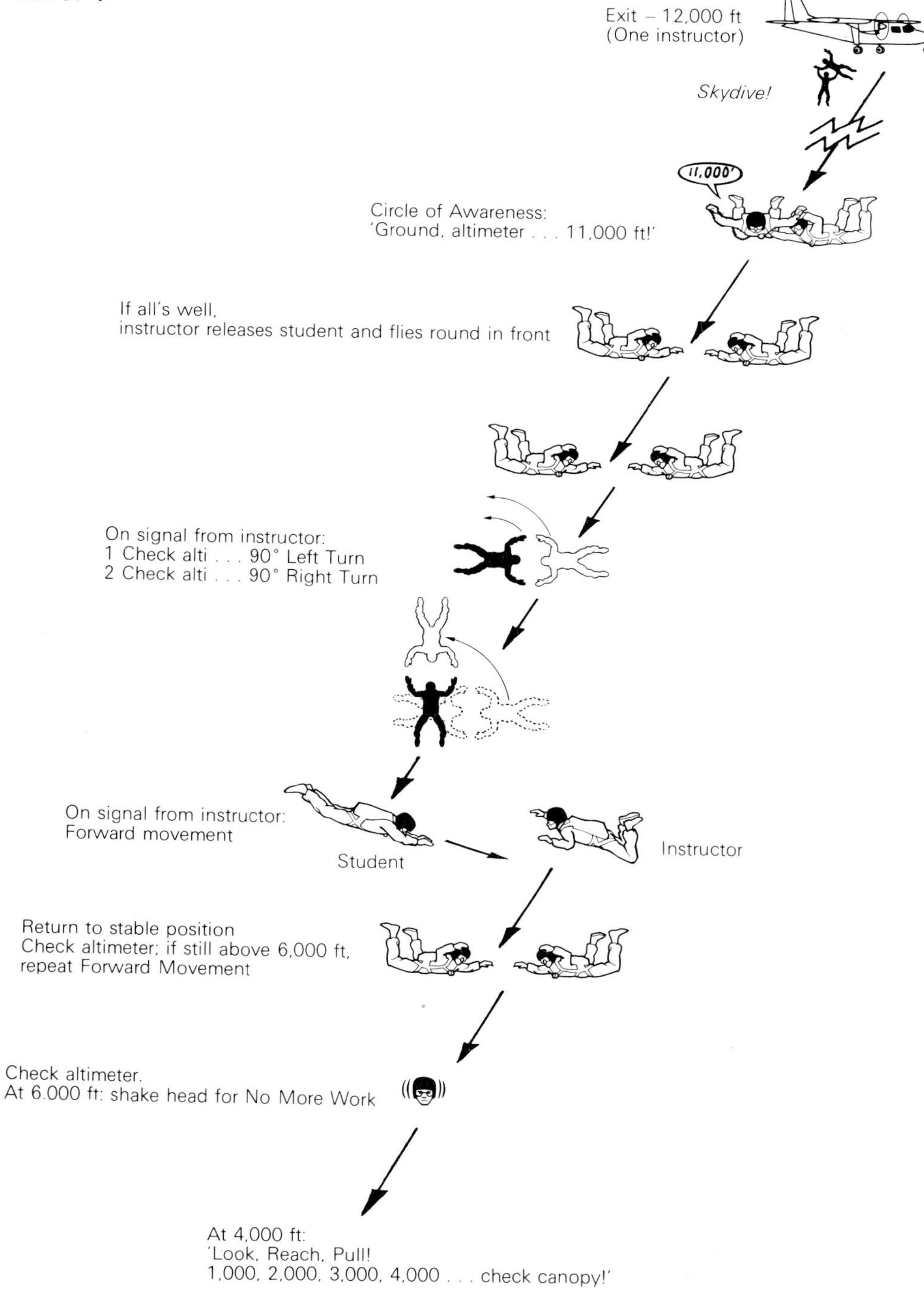
Exit – 12,000 ft
(One instructor)
Skydive!
11,000'
Circle of Awareness:
'Ground, altimeter . . . 11,000 ft!'
If all's well,
instructor releases student and flies round in front
On signal from instructor:
1 Check alti . . . 90° Left Turn
2 Check alti . . . 90° Right Turn
On signal from instructor:
Forward movement
Student
Instructor
Return to stable position
Check altimeter; if still above 6,000 ft,
repeat Forward Movement
Check altimeter.
At 6.000 ft: shake head for No More Work
At 4,000 ft:
'Look, Reach, Pull!
1,000, 2,000, 3,000, 4,000 . . . check canopy!'

black dot was barking a field full of scattered white dots into a tight circle. And to the north, smoke from a field of burning stubble was rising gently in a grey wedge.

Simon was sitting in front of me, singing; Paul Austin, another of the Slipstream instructors, was apparently asleep, resting his head against the fuselage wall, 'Eyes closed, shutters down, sign up, out to lunch.'

I asked Jane to open the door the moment that the plane levelled out, so that I could get used to the change in temperature. And as usual, we went through the checks: harness, attachment points, Cut-away Handle, Main Ripcord Handle, Reserve Handle, belly band, chest band, alti, leg straps, Stephens Lanyard, AAD and finally, the pin.

In 'Relative Work' – the discipline in which human formations are linked together in the sky – the door of an aircraft suddenly seems very small. To get as many people as possible away at the same moment, some members of the group have the unenviable job of climbing out the door and hanging on to the outside of the aircraft by a selection of hand and foot holds. Depending on which part of the outside of the plane you're clinging on to – forward of the door, straight out the door, or aft of the door – the positions are simply known as Front, Centre or Rear Float.

To photograph this jump, Simon Ward was going off Rear Float; so, at 10,000 ft, with an Olympus OM4Ti and Sony Video Camera mounted on his helmet, and the shutter release in his mouth, he climbed out into the storm of the slipstream, and disappeared out of sight.

This time, Jane was hanging out the door in the place that Rod had occupied on all my previous jumps. Now, there was no reassuring face inside the plane, just an empty fuselage. With no one to 'Check In' to, I simply looked out at Jane, now spread-eagled in the doorway with one hand on my leg strap.

'Check Out.'

'Okay!'

'Up, down . . . arch'

I wobbled out sideways into the slipstream and together we tumbled into 10,000 ft of English summer sunshine. The wind blast was quite different; warmer, clearer and not as fierce. And best of all, I felt rock steady.

I shouted the altitude and a moment later, Jane was flying in front of me, with her hand pointing straight-fingered, at my left shoulder. 'Okay,' I thought. 'Left turn . . . *steady* . . . steady . . .' and before I'd moved a muscle, I was pirouetting gently round to the left; as though someone had put out a hand and was spinning me round like the hand on a clock. It was more telepathic than athletic. A very fine adjustment of the shoulders and the turn stopped – I could hardly believe it. A quick altimeter check, and I thought about going back. My right shoulder dropped three inches, and all 200 lbs of me was rotating effortlessly back again.

As soon as I'd reversed the initial 90 degree turn, I was meant to do some forward movement; but I was so chuffed by the success of the first turns, that I took a few more seconds and floated on round for another 90.

From there on down, indeed from the moment we left the aircraft to the Pull, the whole jump seemed to be straight out of the textbook. Even under canopy, I turned into the wind right over the white arrow on the drop zone, drew the steering toggles down to Half Brakes and just enjoyed the view over Cloud Nine.

'Right,' said Jane, hugging a cup of tea with both hands. 'The exit was fine; you gave a little kick, but I let you go immediately because there didn't seem to be any point in hanging on; you were so stable. I wasn't in fact beside you when you shouted out 9,000 ft – I'd already swung round in front of you by then. But that's only a detail. At that stage you may have seen that I had my arms swept right back, almost parallel with my body, which should have told you that you were back-sliding away from me, and I was having to track after you quite hard. The thing is, when you back-slide, you don't just move away; you move *down* and away. If your lower legs are bent right back to your bum, the bottom half of your body is presenting less surface area resistance to the airflow than your top half; which is why you slide away. Anyway, I came down after you and gave you the signal for the left turn. You checked your alti, and off you went.

'And the turns were . . . well, they were perfect,' she said. 'As soon as you'd finished the left and right turns, I saw you going straight into another one, and I guessed you were probably celebrating! After that, you went into the Forward Movement. Now this is important: in those few seconds that you began to straighten out your legs in order to move forward, you didn't straighten them completely; you simply brought them back to where they should be all along. So, in fact, you ended up in the perfect stable position. Eventually, when you *did* straighten them right out, you started coming towards me quite quickly. I think you were probably thinking, in your sub-conscious, "Oh, my God. I'm going to hit her." Well you needn't worry, I'll always get out of your way. Then when you'd flown across to me, your arms went up and your lower legs hinged back to your bum again, and for about three seconds, you did a steep back-slide away from me. Most of the time, though, we were flying nose-to-nose with our fingertips just apart, but not docked. That's what's called 'No Contact Flying', and it's certainly a good sign – we both must have been flying well to do that. Then . . . you shook your head at six grand, which was fine. No problems with the pull and recovery, and I just carried on watching you.'

She thought for a second. 'I'll be honest,' she said, 'it was the best Level IV I've ever seen'.

I was like a dog with two tails.

We watched it on the video. 'You can see that I'm constantly moving,' said Jane, 'I'm adjusting my position very slightly the whole time. That's the thing about flying: you've always got to be prepared for what might be about to happen. You've got to think ahead, anticipate and ease into it. If a turn is speeding up, start correcting in good time and you'll slow it down gradually. If something's happening that you don't want, fight it.'

I was *Cleared to Level V*

Steve and I had now done four jumps each, but our fortunes had changed. I was trying to conceal a glistening ego, and Steve was nursing a dented pride.

Watching the in-flight movie

On this last lift, he'd left the aircraft before me and it hadn't been a good jump.

'We had a stable exit,' he said afterwards, 'and Jack let go of me. The first turn was fine and then, for some reason, I started to wave my right arm slightly. I think Jack realised what I was doing, but before he could do anything, I'd flipped onto my back and did my flailing-arms bit. That was at just over 5,000 ft. Four or five seconds from Pull Time.

'I was tumbling and I was just thinking, "Get stable, get stable." I wasn't aware of the altitude, but obviously Jack was, so he got me in a headlock, grabbed my handle and pulled. For just the last second or so, as the parachute deployed off my back, I was stable again.'

Working out *why* he'd gone unstable wasn't so easy. 'My concentration must have gone,' he said. 'It's like a feeling of panic, a wave of uncertainty comes over me.'

I still hadn't been unstable in a dive, so I couldn't imagine what it felt like to be spinning towards the ground like a human swastika. Steve closed his eyes and shook his head. 'Horrible,' he said. 'Not to be recommended. I felt I had no control at all. And I wasn't thinking of the ground; I just felt absolutely helpless.

'In the stable position, it feels as though you're lying face down on a 6 in. wide plank of wood suspended high above the ground, and you're trying to balance. If you tilt at all, you *know* you're going to fall off – so you start correcting, and that's when I seem to start oscillating. This time, on one of the oscillations, the airflow caught me and flipped me onto my back. It's like a dream; you're not just falling down. It's as though you're twisting and tumbling down a huge tunnel. You can't do anything, that's the feeling. But this time I was thinking, "Sod off, Jack. I want to do it myself." Luckily, he didn't.

Steve and I had both learnt that the stable or 'face-to-earth' position was the key to confidence. 'If I knew I could get stable *and* get the concentration. That really is the sticking point – the fear of going unstable.'

He also felt that he needed the maximum altitude for the next few jumps. All of the jumps on the course are done from above 9,000 ft but because of air traffic control, it isn't always possible to get clearance to 12,000 ft, the maximum jump altitude for AFF. 'Even ten grand is too low at the moment,' he said. 'I just have the feeling in the back of my mind that I'm working with reduced height.'

With the possibility of an AFF student tumbling

chaotically through the sky, it isn't surprising that national parachuting associations around the world demand such exceptional standards in skydiving and teaching skills before awarding an Instructor his or her AFF rating. To be eligible for the AFF Instructor course in the first place, a candidate must already be a Static Line Instructor – with proven teaching ability – and have at least 1,000 jumps and ten hours in freefall to their credit. At the end of the course, the student instructors have to do a total of five jumps with their examiners.

'For example,' Jane explained, 'the examiner may say, "Right, you're doing Primary Jumpmaster on a Level III." Then he'll just say, "Time In" and from that moment on, he becomes a student. Which means, naturally, that they'll do all the usual things that a typical student might do on the ground and in the air.

'You can score up to four points on each jump: zero is unsatisfactory and four is very good. Over the five jumps a successful candidate must get 12 points or more out of 20. There are no second chances or rejumps, and if you miss out a *single* safety point, you automatically get zero for that jump. The "student" may kit himself up properly and so on, but if you forget to check his pin or Automatic Actuation Device, it won't matter how well you perform in the air after that, he still won't give you a point. The same goes for something like allowing him to walk too close to a propeller.'

Jane admits that the responsibility is enormous. 'But as an instructor, you expect to take responsibility, it's a responsible job. It's just that AFF demands even more of you, because you're actually out in freefall with the student.'

Newcomers to AFF, though, are left in no doubt as to where the final responsibility lies. 'On every AFF jump', said Jane, 'the responsibility is still the student's own, simply because they're trained and have their own parachutes. But obviously, it's up to the instructor not to progress a student to the next level if they think he isn't ready for it.'

Pete Gannaw was listening to Jane and smiling.

'You know, there was a video I saw once, about a girl they nicknamed Helicopter Annie. And I still think it should be shown to every AFF Instructor as a reminder to be careful up there.

'These two big guys, her instructors, were 200 lbs each. But Helicopter Annie wasn't even a hundred pounds. She was on a release dive (Level III) and as soon as they let her go, she stayed there, in the stable position, for about three seconds and then off she went: into-it and out-of-it, into-it and out-of-it. And you know, these guys could really fly; one of 'em had well over 3,000 jumps at that time, and the other guy had around 2,000. They'd get a hold of her and she'd kick 'em right off. Man, she was all over the sky. Apparently, she'd been a pretty good student, but she just went nuts. She'd come through that thing spinnin' sometimes.

'In the end,' he says, 'the role of the instructor is more like that of a doctor. He figures out the student's problem, diagnoses it, prescribes a cure, then administers the treatment. And that may be five rejumps at one level – the instructor always has the choice.'

From now on, altitude awareness would be completely up to me. I wouldn't have to shout out the altitude to Jane. 'I'll release you after the exit,' said Jane, 'and then I'll come round in front, just like last time.'

Instead of doing 90 degree left and right turns, I'd be doing two 360 degree turns – effectively going round the dark side of the moon.

'When you've done those,' said Jane, 'we'll aim to do a re-dock; which means you'll actually fly back towards me and take a grip on me.'

From there on, it would be exactly the same as before. A shake of the head at 6,000 ft for 'No More Work', with the Pull at 4,000 ft.

The docking, or 'pinning' as it's sometimes known, was going to be an intimate affair. 'What we have to do,' Jane explained, 'is fly together so that our noses are almost touching, with our arms spread as they would be in the normal stable position. That means straightening your legs right out, moving your arms back a little; and you'll fly in towards me, so that we're flying No Contact. Then you take a grip on my shoulders, but without reaching forward for it – your arms should stay in the same position, you should only have to close your hands to take the grip. Then when you've taken hold of my shoulders, just think about raising your lower legs again slightly. There shouldn't be any tension in the grip. When you let go again, we should both stay exactly where we are – rather than moving apart or whatever.'

Then it was a shake of the head and back to alti checks, until the Pull – this time with a slight variation. 'Just before the Pull,' said Jane, 'I want you to bring your arms across your head like a pair of scissors and do what we call a "Wave Off". That's simply preparing you for Relative Work which you'll get on to when you've qualified. You're just warning

Top No Contact Flying made easy at an altitude of 2ft.

Above Practising the Cutaway drills: 'Look, Reach, Pull. . . Malfunction! :'PEEL' off the cutaway pad, 'PULL' it to cut away the main canopy, and 'PUNCH' the Reserve handle away.

anyone who may be above you that you're about to pull. If a large formation is breaking up, everyone always does a Wave Off before turning away from the centre of the formation, and then tracking away to get some space to deploy.'

In the afternoon, the sky was filled with small white flak bursts of cloud, low and fast moving. Without the breeze – which was just over the top for skydiving – it would have been the sort of balmy summer day that everyone happily imagines English summers are made of.

For the first time, I was positively looking forward

to leaving that aircraft and relaxing, flexibly, into the stable position. It seemed to be largely a matter of taking control of the airflow around you.

Four hours later, the poplar trees were still bending along the edge of the airfield. To make matters worse, the weekend build up of jumpers had begun: five tandem students and several AFF Level I students had arrived at the Slipstream office, hoping to do their one jump for Cancer Research and for Great Ormond Street Hospital. By 2030 – and I hesitate to admit it – I was thoroughly bored. How could it be possible, I wondered, to experience total exhilaration and rank boredom in the same afternoon?

Below Until you're fully qualified, your parachute will always be packed by an instructor.

☐ Parachuting pilots
☐ Learning to wait
☐ France's skydiving restaurateur
☐ Restrictions on age?
☐ Twelve hours of frustation

DAY SIX

At 0830, the airfield was covered in wall-to-wall grey clouds at around 5,000 ft. It was a different place. Fifty more students were wandering around, waiting to be marshalled for their weekend First Jump Course on static line.

Already, the noise was building up in the canteen and the surest sign that the weather wasn't all it might be – the warm smell of toast and bacon – was pouring from its windows. Maureen, affectionately regarded as part of the airfield furniture, was busily emptying ashtrays into a black plastic bag and wiping the tables with a very tired cloth. I wondered what she thought of parachutists.

'Oh, they've got worse,' she said.

'Worse than when?'

She put her hands on her broad hips, and two faces behind the serving area rolled their eyes. 'Well, it never used to be like this,' she said. 'It's only since the parachutists started here. It just used to be a small place, just at weekends at first, and then they started coming in during the week as well. I mean, just look at it,' she said, waving her cloth at the torn, padded seats where large areas of foam-rubber was now visible, exposed by nervous and impatient fingers.

'It'd make your heart break, wouldn't it?'

But if this was a woman with the problems of the world on her shoulders, she wasn't going to let it get her down. 'They may think I'm a fusser, but oh no,' she said, 'they can't twist me, I know a thing or two.'

I didn't think they'd dare. 'Surely they're not such a bad lot?'

She gave me a world-weary look. 'I've just told you,' she said, 'they're animals.'

Outside, a small boy was having trouble reading the sign marking the Whuffo Line to his little sister.

'No Dogs, No Kids and No . . . um, Wives Beyond This Point'

I was just about to explain to him that the world was, in fact, split into two kinds of people, when Jane arrived. There were plenty of whuffos around today.

'Yeah,' said Jane, 'and a few Splinkies as well.'

'Splinkies?'

'Well, you often get girls hanging round drop zones, looking for men. They're called Splinkies. I don't know why.'

In fact, there is one other species in the skydiving world, and it no longer seems to surprise them that they're so often forgotten. A spoof *A–Z of Parachute Jargon* in a recent issue of *The Sport Parachutist* arrived at this definition:

'PILOT: That useless, slack-jawed cretin at the front of the plane.'

Skydivers and pilots seem to maintain a healthy and light-hearted disrespect for each other. But whatever they may say, for someone like 22 year-old Shaun Whitling, parachute flying is still an enjoyable way for a young pilot to build up flying hours. As one of several regular jump pilots at Headcorn, he has spent around 600 hours in the last year at the controls of the club's Islanders. When he first came to Headcorn, his attitude, as a pilot, was that anybody who jumps out of planes was totally mad.

'I told them, they'd never get me doing it.'

But they did.

'They gave me an AFF Level I jump for my 21st birthday, last year. And it was the most exhilarating thing I've ever done. I'd liked to have carried on, but there just hasn't been time.'

The worst bit, he says, was putting the kit on. 'But once I'd walked out to the aeroplane, that was it. It was so different sitting in the *back* of the plane knowing that I was going to jump out. Now I can see that there's nothing wrong with it. I see everyone climbing out behind me and having such a good time.

'Skydivers think pilots are bad news,' he said. 'They don't care much for the pilots. You can sit in the plane for eight hours and no one'll even bring you a cup of tea. When they get in the aeroplane, some of them can be a bit mouthy. Or they're frustrated because the weather's bad, and they can't get up. Often they'll want to know what the weather's going to do and then I get all sorts of stick if I'm wrong.

'Some of them are very full of "Go for it", even if it's blowing 29 knots. But I've still got to say, "Sorry we can't do it", because both my neck and the Chief Instructor's neck are on the block if anything goes wrong.'

It wasn't all bad. 'No,' he said, 'on the ground they're wonderful people; down the pub . . . great.'

The sky was looking steadily more impenetrable. 'Well it doesn't matter what the weather does for the next hour,' said Shaun. 'London Air Traffic Control have a computer failure, so they won't be able to issue us with a squawk until at least 1100. And we can't go above 5,500 ft until they have it sorted out.'

'A squawk?'

'Yeah, that's simply a number we get issued with by London ATC every day. We just feed it into the aircraft's transponder, and it provides West Drayton with a continuous update on the aeroplane's position and altitude.'

Jack was lining up the clouds against the corner of a building. 'Think its gonna break up? I'm not very current on British weather.'

I didn't think so. In between the rain showers there was time for some dirt dives, but still the waiting went on.

No one seems to have come up with anything very constructive to do in order to pass the time when the weather is bad. Gradually I came to understand why. I tried reading, first newspapers, then books and magazines. I tried eating eggs and bacon, salad rolls and cheeseburgers; and drinking cups of tea and coffee, coke and lemonade. I even tried to sleep. But in the end, I realised that it just isn't possible to relax completely. The chance of getting a lift, particularly between showers on a marginal day like this, is still so imminent that you don't want to be scrambling for the plane without having had time to re-gather your thoughts.

Andy Ring was lying in a deck chair, eyes closed behind a pair of Elvis Costello sunglasses.

'Do people get better at waiting?'

'No,' he said. 'In fact, the irony of it is that the longer you're kept on the ground, the sooner people start to get injured. A bloke injured his back badly the other day jumping over a fence; and a first-timer was carried off with a sprained ankle while playing volleyball. And then, of course, there was the time we started playing "Catch" at 50 yards with a coconut; that was a broken finger.'

An invisible plane was moaning high overhead, near the edge of a black cloud that was about to deliver another shower. The aircraft appeared briefly and then was lost again.

'I still don't think they'll get it in,' someone said. 'They're on the Run In, so they're going to be dumping in cloud if they get out there.'

'What would happen if they deployed in that sort of cloud?'

'Well sometimes you can go up to flippin' . . . well, however high the top of the cloud is. You can go straight up inside it'.

'It actually lifts you up?'

'Yeah,' he said. 'We've had some people go up 15,000 ft in cloud.'

'The record,' said Andy, pointing at the black cloud, 'is someone who opened in front of one of those buggers and landed 60 miles away.'

Among the newly-graduated AFF students waiting for a jump was John Irvine, a tall big-jawed Ulsterman, dressed in the skydivers unofficial uniform of T-shirt, tracksuit trousers and trainers. 'It's funny,' he said, 'sometimes you're relieved you're not jumping; and other times, you can't wait to get up there. I used to really go by the weather forecast; if I heard that it was going to be bad, I wouldn't bother driving down. But then I'd hear the next day that they'd had about 10 lifts. I find the forecast tells you whether it's going to be generally good, or generally bad. There are usually some good patches even on the worst days; but that's just the sport in this country.'

In the afternoon, another light aircraft joined the ranks on the edge of the airfield. Its pilot and owner, who has the distinction of being the oldest AFF student yet trained at Headcorn, is a charming and resolute little Frenchman with close-cropped silver hair. For the last 17 years, Henri Bouqiere has owned a restaurant – *The Stag* – in the City of London. His first jump, on the static line course, had been a 62nd birthday present the year before.

One jump had been enough for the skydiving bug to grab him firmly between its teeth, and after just a few weeks on the conventional training course, he swapped to Accelerated Freefall. When he joined us in the Slipstream Office, it was clear that he'd made the change for the same reason as everyone else.

'I just got fed up with all the Static Line jumps,' he said. 'You see, I deedn't 'ave a lot of time to do all zat training, and I wanted to get on.'

As it happened, even his AFF training took a little longer than average; but not because of his age. As a former French National high-board diving champion he was finding it difficult not to go out the door of the aircraft in a faultless swallow dive. 'Being a diver, you don't associate bending ze legs on ze dive. You keep your legs straight.'

He stood on his tip toes. 'You know, it's stretch . . . stretch. Maybe a very slight arch. But parachutists muss be the opposite way. I had a lot of problems at all levels.'

Unfortunately, faultless swallow dives out of an aircraft door have a fairly devastating effect on your ability to get stable. Henri spent much of his time doing an impression of a oak seedling in a high wind. Fortunately, he'd arranged for all his jumps to be filmed, and an appropriate soundtrack had been added, so that his tiny red figure came tumbling and turning out the door to the trickling melodies of a French café accordian.

I wondered what his friends and indeed his customers would say if they could see this effervescent little Parisian exchanging his black tie for a green jumpsuit, and plummeting to earth at 120 mph.

'Well dey don' realise. I mean, you know, dey juss say, "You muss be mad", which is probably right. My waff 'as never come down 'ere. Of course, she 'as seen my video. But it dezzen mean anyzing to 'er.'

Playing patience

'And is she quite happy about you skydiving?'

'Oh yes, I've been doing so many sports now that she dezzen care: water ski, snow ski, badminton, windsurfing, gliding, and flying, which is my sport actually.'

Henri is a good example of why there shouldn't be an upper age limit for skydiving. As Jane, who was his Primary Instructor, explained, 'When a student is a bit older, we have to be even more careful because their reactions are slower. Obviously, Henri's very fit: you wouldn't consider taking someone of that age through the course if they weren't. In his case, he already holds a Private Pilot's Licence and he's had to have a very strict medical for that.

'In fact, Henri, ended up doing three Level IIIs, not just because his body position wasn't right, but because he wasn't showing us awareness; he wasn't reading his altimeter and we were having to remind him where 5,000 ft was. He ended up doing those three rejumps for that reason alone.'

All day, the cloud base varied between 3,500–5,000 ft. High enough to allow the Static Line jumpers to carry on tumbling out all day. But for AFF, Saturday was a 12 hour wash-out.

- ☐ Level 5, at last
- ☐ Turning full circle
- ☐ High altitude link up
- ☐ Preparing for Level 6 (Solo Exit, Backloops and Tracking)
- ☐ The secret of Steve's success
- ☐ Rain stops play

DAY SEVEN

It was now exactly 48 hours since I'd done my last jump. Long enough to have me pacing up and down, whispering and walking my way through the sequence of the next dive. Levels IV and V tend to be sticking points for many AFF students, and after two days without a jump, even I couldn't be sure any more that my Level IV hadn't been a fluke.

Meanwhile, the first-time static liners were sitting bum-to-bum on the benches by the Manifest Hut, smiling nervously. Instructors were fussing around them, tugging at tabs and checking them over.

'The sad thing,' says Jane, 'is that most of these students will only ever make that first jump, and they'll say, "I've parachuted". In fact, they've really only scratched the surface of the sport; many of them don't realise that they could move on to freefall.'

When the weather is good, the two Islanders spend very little time on the ground. Jumpers for the next lift simply walk out and stand at the edge of the airstrip, where someone has thoughtfully installed a Kent County Council Bus Stop. That was where we were waiting at 1130, when *Juliet Echo* taxied over, and we climbed in behind the spinning props.

We fell away from the aircraft as normal but by now, my eyes and ears had begun to take the whole business in their stride. I tensed just for a second or two as we wallowed in the wind, and then relaxed. This time, I

Level 5

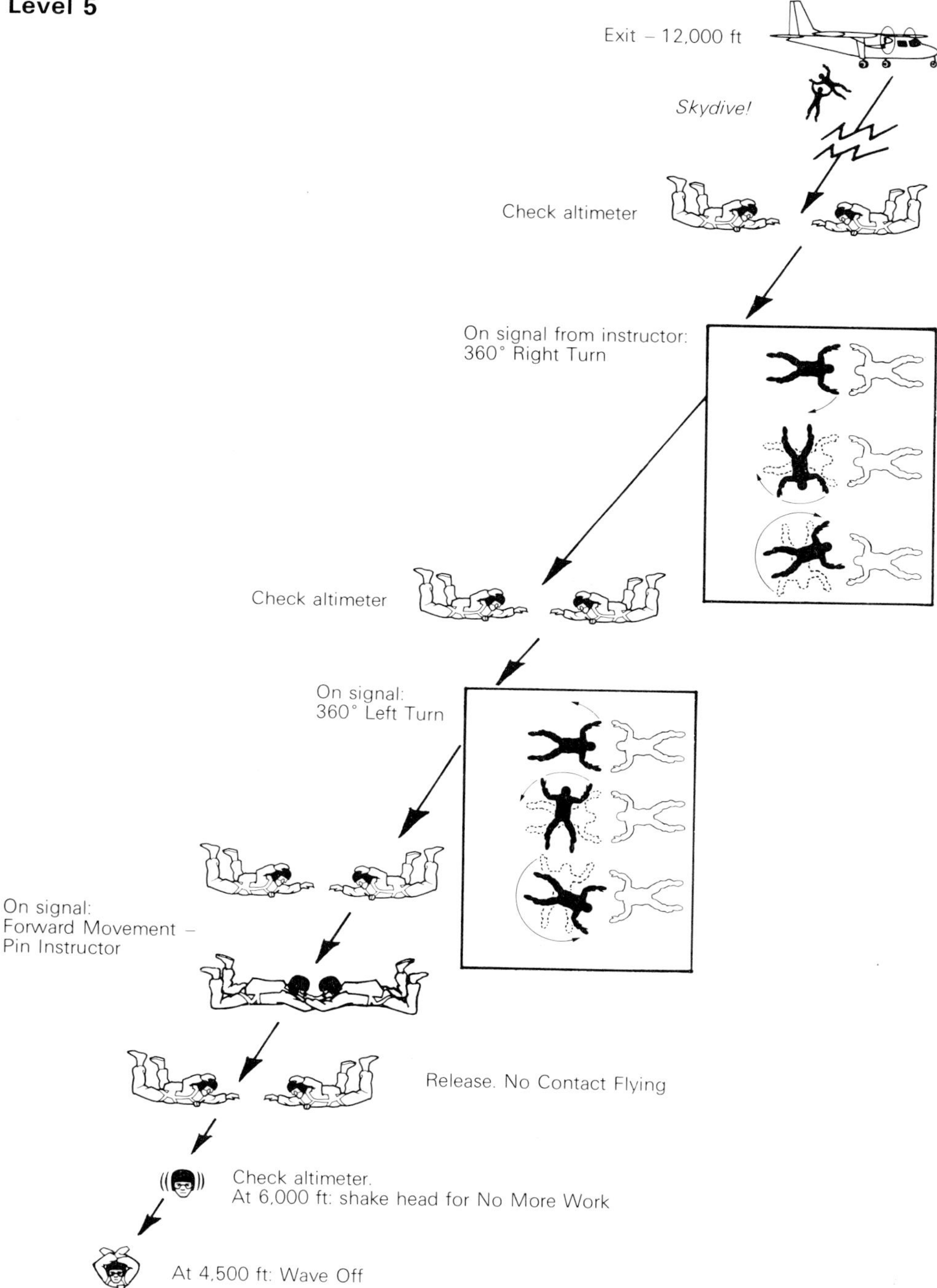

'Look, Reach, Pull!
1,000, 2,000, 3,000, 4,000 . . . check canopy!'

was determined to be firm with my lower legs, and obediently, they assumed the correct position. Soon, Jane and I were flying face to face, vertically down the tube.

I went into the first 360 degree turn very, very gradually. It was like lying at the centre of a giant record player. Halfway through the first turn at a sedate 33 rpm, I was staring at empty sky without a sign of life, and then, a second later, Jane's fluttering face re-appeared over my left shoulder. A quick check on the altitude and then I went into auto-reverse; a tiny left-shoulder-up, right-shoulder-down movement, this time at 45 rpm. I still hadn't the faintest idea what point of the compass I was flying on, but from Jane's position, I knew when the turn was complete.

I looked down into the stream of wind and noise. Small fields were expanding alarmingly into large fields. The whole patchwork of land, or as much of it as my eyes was allowing me to take in, was roaring towards us. But the hand on the dial on my chest had only just swept past 8,000 ft.

The next movement felt as close to human flight as I suppose I'll ever come. Jane was 8 ft from me. My legs went down; my arms came back and the gap narrowed until we were literally face to face, nose to nose. I closed my hands on her shoulder grips and we were linked for perhaps three seconds. Just long enough to hear Jane screaming sweet nothings in my ear.

With that, my lower legs flipped up again and I felt myself backslide violently, chest up for a second. I let go and then came level again.

If I'd known how to, I'd have done a victory roll, but instead I contented myself with another blissfully uninhibited scream. Jane's expression was saying, 'Well go on then, do it again.' So I did.

Seven seconds later, we were at 6,500 ft. A shake of the head and then, for a whole ten seconds I watched the ground, spellbound by the changing shapes. The Wave Off came at 4,500, '*Look, Reach, Pull . . .*' and I kept my teeth firmly clenched together for the count.

The debrief took just five minutes.

'Just one thing,' said Jane. 'Remember I told you not to let your legs come right back suddenly as soon as you've gripped me? Well, that's exactly what happened, and instantly I felt the tension; your legs tucked up, the back end of your body went down and I could feel you pulling me. Apart from that, it was great. Level VI next, and if you can crack that, the rest is easy.'

We looked at the video and even Jane couldn't

work out how I was managing to turn. There was still no visible movement in my shoulders. But I seemed to be stopping it by cocking one leg slightly, like an airborne labrador.

'That doesn't matter,' she said. 'Your turns are good. Whatever you're doing, it's working. It's not exactly how we teach it, but it's right for you.'

That seems to be the case with most people. Having learnt how turns *should* be done, you'll teeter round in your own way, and gradually refine the movement with practice. The only lesson I learnt was simply to ease into it very gently.

A few seconds before the end of the video, I left the top of the frame as my main parachute deployed. Simon carried on down, so that Jane could demonstrate a backloop, blowing a kiss to the camera as her parachute deployed.

Headcorn was still baking under a hot sun and I was over the moon.

Cleared to Level VI

Now, for the first time, I was going to be leaving the aircraft unattached to another human being – another example of how I was gradually accepting suggestions that would have seemed unthinkable a few days before.

We went round to the mock-up. This time, my hands would no longer be placed on top of one another at the edge of the door; instead, my right hand would be on the floor beside me, with the left hand on the rear side of the doorway behind me.

'Now this time, when you arch,' said Jane, 'you should be lifting your weight onto your right arm and actually levering yourself out into the slipstream, facing straight into it. It should be even easier to get stable. Without anyone holding onto you, you can judge your entry into the slipstream more easily, and it'll be hitting you straight on, on the chest.'

She was sitting in the doorway of the mock up. 'So it's, "Up, Down, Arch" as usual, but as you leave, look up. When we're well away from the aircraft in freefall, we're face-to-earth. But for the first few seconds after we leave the door of the plane, we're met, first of all by what's called the relative wind of the slipstream which comes down off the wings at about 45 degrees. So, look up; you want to be slightly chest up in the slipstream – properly presented to it. Then as you come down off the slipstream, you'll come horizontal into the stable or face-to-earth position.'

The Solo Seated Exit: 'It's more of an entry into the slipstream than an exit from the aircraft'.

I asked her what people tended to get wrong at this level – and rather wished I hadn't.

'Well,' she said, 'the commonest thing is when people don't get their chest into the slipstream. Or, because there's no one holding onto them, they kick and thrash. Or else they go out de-arched – in other words, without arching enough – and immediately they go onto their back.'

Terrific.

'But if that happens, don't panic. Just push out the arch.'

We ran through it.

'Check In'

'Okay'

'Up, down . . . hard arch.' I jumped out, feet apart on the concrete, with my arms in a Y above my head.

'Now look up,' said Jane, 'You should aim to watch the aircraft going away from you.'

'Right, that's the exit. Now the backloop.' This was one of the more difficult exercises to demonstrate on the ground. But the frame-by-frame video gave a very good idea of what was involved.

'Your arms are going to give you the sideways stability so that you don't tumble left or right as you're going into the loop. So you straighten them out and move them slightly forward. At the same time, bring your knees up to your chest; and you can see that as soon as you do that, you're losing the lift from the back end of the body, with lots still on the forward end. That'll push you over into a back somersault – or what we call a backloop.

'As your legs come over your head, keep your head back, and as soon as you see the ground coming round, arch. It should take about three seconds; it's not a violent movement, but at the same time, it's not a slow, ponderous movement. You have to be positive.'

I was having trouble working out which way I'd be going over – forwards or backwards.

'The easiest way to think about it, is that you're throwing your legs over your head.'

'Now . . . tracking.'

This was certainly a rapid progression course. 'Right,' she said, 'you're in the stable position. And the thing is, just as before, go into it slowly. Don't rush it. Remember what Rod was saying: slow is smooth and smooth is fast. It's just like forward movement: the legs straighten right out, but instead of moving your arms back slightly, you sweep them back on the same level as your body – like the first part of the breaststroke movement in swimming, but with the palms still face to earth. In fact you sweep your arms right round until they're almost parallel with your body, still with the palms of your hands facing down.

'You're going to be a bit head-down in the track; and the main thing to remember is that if you go into it too fast, you'll track too steeply and you'll roll over.'

As I'd said to Steve, I still hadn't been unstable yet. But it sounded as though there'd be plenty of opportunity to try some unplanned sky-waltzes on this one.

'You don't want to be arching your spine too hard in the track,' said Jane, because 'that'll make you buffet and probably turn. You want to be dead flat. You've really got to point your toes, and feel as though your forcing everything out through them. And keep your head up. Before you go into the track, though, you should pick up a heading on the ground, so you've got a reference point.

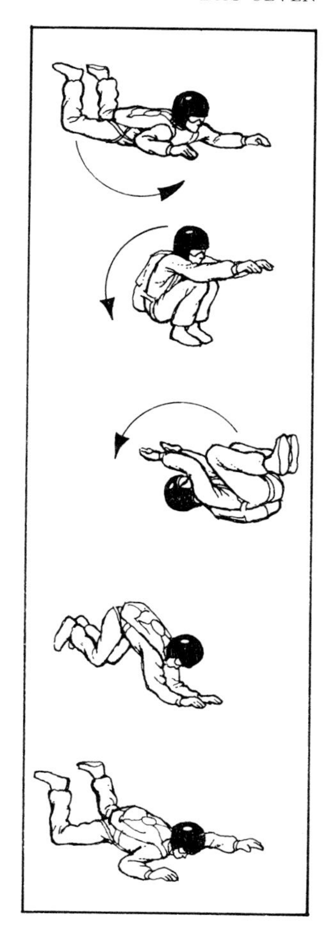

The Backloop: Falling heels over head

'Now just imagine you're tracking down at about 45 degrees . . . if all's going well, all I want you to do is lean slightly and change your heading. You've really just made yourself into an arrow, and changing your direction in the track only needs a very slight movement. When you flare out into the stable position again, you mustn't do it too suddenly, or you'll just sit up and flip over backwards. In a real "max-track", which you'll learn later on, you actually stick your bum up slightly to make yourself into an aerofoil.

'Now,' she said, 'the only thing we've really got to look at is altitudes.' Depending on what height we were cleared for, we'd have to alter the exercise. If I was able to start the track at 9,000 ft or higher, I'd be able to hold it for around ten seconds. 'And if we're only just above 6,000 ft then you'll only have four or five seconds.'

In the stable position, the human body will fall at around 120 mph, but tracking downwards at an angle, wind resistance is reduced and speeds of up to 200 mph can be achieved.

Because my altitude awareness had been good, Jane gave me a cut off or No More Work height of 5,000 ft with the pull at 3,500 ft.

We went through it again and again.

Meanwhile, Steve had finally succeeded in cracking Level IV – his left and right turns – on his third re-jump.

'Brilliant,' he said, 'absolutely brilliant.'

But what had he done differently? 'Well, I think I just took my time and thought about it a bit more in the air. And I'll be honest, I was absolutely bricking it on the way up to the jump altitude; I was far more terrified than on my first jump, simply because I was so frightened of tumbling about and cocking it up. I gave a little kick before I got into the arch and thought, "Oh God, here I am again". But I reported 11,500 ft to Jack and he flew round in front of me. He couldn't signal to me with his hands because he was holding me, so he stuck his tongue out at me which meant Straighten Legs. And that was fine. Then he released me and all my mental energy was spent on keeping my body in *exactly* the same position. Apparently, Jack gave me a little twist because I had a slight lean. But I drifted quite happily round to the right and then the left on my 360s; it went like a dream.'

The secret, he discovered, was just *thinking in the*

Level 6

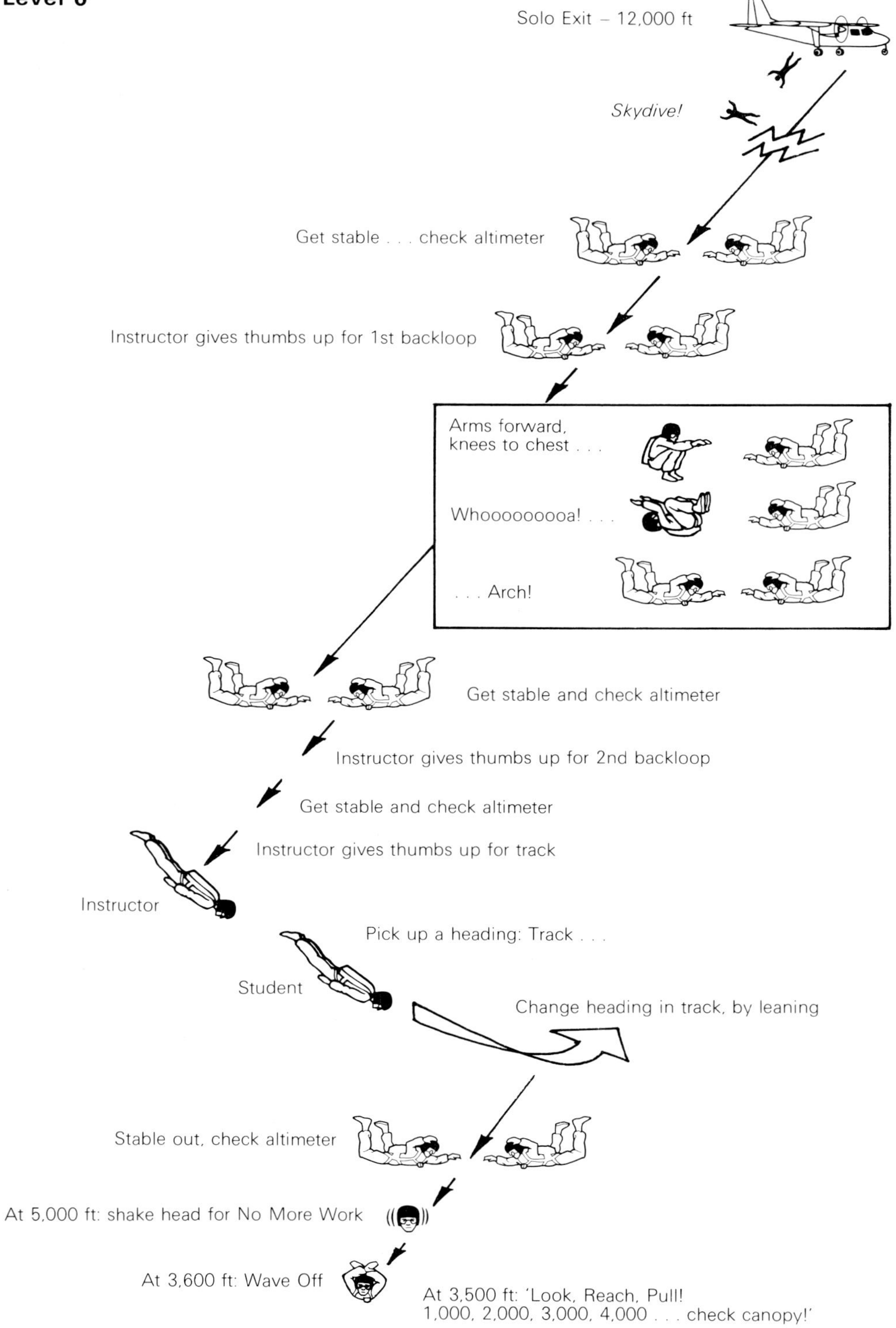
Solo Exit – 12,000 ft
Skydive!
Get stable . . . check altimeter
Instructor gives thumbs up for 1st backloop
Arms forward, knees to chest . . .
Whooooooooa! . . .
. . . Arch!
Get stable and check altimeter
Instructor gives thumbs up for 2nd backloop
Get stable and check altimeter
Instructor gives thumbs up for track
Instructor
Pick up a heading: Track . . .
Student
Change heading in track, by leaning
Stable out, check altimeter
At 5,000 ft: shake head for No More Work
At 3,600 ft: Wave Off
At 3,500 ft: 'Look, Reach, Pull! 1,000, 2,000, 3,000, 4,000 . . . check canopy!'

air. 'You have to think actively, "What next? Steady . . ." and then go into it.

'I just thought to myself, "Don't you dare do anything remotely unstabilising!" I just relaxed and took it all gently.'

By mid-afternoon, the cloudbase showed no sign whatever of lifting. Overhead, every now and then, the engines of the two Islanders were still being suddenly throttled back, allowing their loads of static line students to yell their way out into the slipstream at 2,000 ft. But still, AFF jumps were clearly not in the script.

Two hours later it was raining in that steady old pitter-patter that goes on for hour after hour. And the sky was echoing with deep intestinal noises. Two large holes in the clouds, each a couple of miles wide, slipped by without a flicker of sunshine.

'It doesn't matter how far you can see above the airfield,' said Shaun Whitling. 'We've got to be able to see those hills – about three miles – before we're allowed to jump.'

Just when it started to clear up a bit, a voice came over the tannoys. It was Chris Francis. 'I'm afraid that one of the Islanders – *Juliet Echo* – is now out of action with an oil problem. So we're restricted to one aircraft for the rest of the day.'

Seven jumps in seven days had brought my total Time in Freefall to a respectable 5 minutes 45 seconds. I still had three more levels to do and with boundless optimism, I only had one morning left to do them.

DAY EIGHT

- ☐ Morbid curiosity
- ☐ Coming to terms with bouncing
- ☐ Level 6: six seconds as a human missile
- ☐ Over-confidence brings an undignified landing
- ☐ Preparing for Level 7 (Dive Exit)
- ☐ Head first and a late pull
- ☐ Flying alone (Level 8) and Graduation

On the morning that I'd started the course, the *Daily Star* had given its entire front page to a skydiving story. Splashed across its tabloid cover were the words: 'FLY HIGH JACQUI'.

Above the headline was a photograph of a smiling girl, freefalling in tandem with an instructor. Twenty-five year old Jacqui Harper – a thalidomide victim with no legs – had already raised £23,000 for a brain-damaged baby. This time, she'd done a tandem jump and was quoted as saying, 'It was fantastic. I think everyone should have a go. It's like nothing else in the world.' It was a rare piece of good PR for the sport.

But now, a week later, the papers were carrying a very different story. It was about another young girl – 21 year-old Paula Goodayle – whose parachute had been blown off course, carrying her down on to the blades of a helicopter which was hovering six feet above the ground.

Over and above the horrific death that she had suffered, much was made of the fact that this – her first and only jump – had been intended to raise money for her grandfather who was dying of cancer. It was difficult to avoid it as a topic of conversation, particularly, when a film crew and reporters arrived at Headcorn to do a story on skydiving and safety. At the same time, MPs were calling for a ban on charity jumps. One had even been reported as saying, 'Clubs and instructors must be licensed – at the moment, parachuting is not adventure, it's sheer murder.' It was unusual to be in the position to realise what an ill-informed judgement that had been.

By a rather morbid irony, press reports of parachuting deaths often increase rather than decrease the number of calls to parachute centres around the country. Although on the face of it, the weight of people will be less inclined to try the sport as a result, it seems to bring parachuting far enough into the public eye to attract a new batch of beginners. As Debbie Allum, one of the partners of Slipstream explained, 'We get callers every day who say things like, "I'd like to make a parachute jump. How safe is it? What are my chances of dying?" – especially after there's been a fatality.'

This pattern isn't peculiar to the United Kingdom. 'When I was running the student programme in Z-hills,' said Jack Gregory, 'there only had to be the smallest incident in the press or on television in Florida, and there'd be a marked increase in the number of calls. That's how we get most of our students. I'm serious.'

Did he know exactly why? 'Advertising,' he declared. 'It's as simple as that. Maybe it just makes people wonder, "Gee, I wonder what it is about skydiving that would make a person take the chance. Maybe there's something there." But it's all advertising. "It doesn't matter what they say as long as they spell the name right" – that's so true.'

Jack came to terms with this question a long time ago. 'We had a fatality one time at Zephyr Hills,' he remembers. 'It was during a very busy time and a person was killed. Okay, we took care of the matter and I was back at the drop zone within an hour, when I'd done whatever I could. So I came back, and we were still skydiving. Then a reporter asked me, "*Why* are these people skydiving?" And I said, "You can't just stop living", and I asked him whether he'd ever had a friend killed in a car accident. He said that he had, so I asked him how he'd got to the funeral. He stopped for a moment, and then he said, "You're right, I took a car."' Jack shook his head. 'And that's it, you *can't* just stop living.'

Since dawn, vapour trails had been darning the holes in the cloud cover. There was only a whisper of a breeze from the north-east and it was looking good for jumping.

At 1100, we were climbing over Headcorn in a cold clear sky. Beside me in the aircraft was a thin-faced Canadian skydiver in a bright yellow jumpsuit who was 'doing' England with his wife. In the casual way that travelling skydivers do, he'd simply decided to fit in a jump on his way through Kent. Now, for the first time, I was sitting close enough to the open door to watch each jumper *after* they'd left the aircraft. So when, at 7,000 ft, the yellow figure beside me climbed into the doorway, I poked my head out into the slipstream.

From the stable platform of the aircraft, I watched him disappear like the dot in the centre of an old television screen. At first, he fell terrifyingly quickly, like a yellow rag doll, until quite suddenly he vanished among the fields. Then, a second later, a bright red canopy erupted a long way behind us.

When our turn came, Jane didn't bother with the formal invitation to skydive, instead she shouted, 'Let's go and boogie!'

Perched in the doorway, this time without a single hand on any of my seven handles. I began to sympathise with Humpty Dumpty. There didn't seem to be any point in dawdling, so I went straight into it, pushing off sideways into the windblast. I left the aircraft and the cold wave of the slipstream hit me square in the chest and the last thing I saw before I levelled out was the aircraft going away, with Jane tumbling out the door above me.

'Backloops are easy,' someone had said, 'providing that you go into them positively.' And they were. But when it came to it, they were over so quickly that I hardly knew they'd happened at all. One moment, you're plummeting, frog-like in the approved stable position, then you make a conscious decision to push your arms out further and bring your knees up. Something happens very suddenly, three seconds later it stops, and your legs are back where they started. Again, it requires total concentration on what your various limbs are about to do. So total, in fact, that for those few seconds you forget completely that you're falling to earth at 120 mph. Best of all, you come out of it feeling like you've just completed a successful re-entry from outer space.

At 9,500 ft, Jane gave me the thumbs up for the second one. Arms out, knees to chest, head back and again, there was a blur of green, a blur of blue and another blur of green which settled again into landscape.

Jane was still making rude faces at me; so I pulled my *No Sex Please, We're British* face, turned through 90 degrees, lined myself up on a railway line, straightened out into an arrow and accelerated down an invisible ramp.

I'd have done the whole week's training for thos
next six seconds alone.

Already, in eight days, falling had become just tha
a fairly inevitable consequence of jumping out of
plane. But tracking . . . that required a positive an
completely independent decision in the air. For si
seconds, I rocketed head down like a human missile.
I'd only known before-hand what it was going to fee
like, I'd have bought myself a royal blue jump suit,
red cape and a pair of scarlet underpants, specially fo
the occasion.

I'd picked up a heading, but I still hadn't a clu
whether it was north, south, east or west. I buffetec
straightened, buffeted and straightened again and b
then it seemed a good idea to stop. I just let the win
take my arms and legs back into the stable, frog-in
mid-leap position.

It was still only 6,000 ft, so I slotted in a quick 36
degree turn to the right. If someone had told me
week earlier that I'd be deciding calmly to do 36
degree turns just 25 seconds from impact, I wouldn'
have believed them. Ten seconds later, at 5,000 ft
there wasn't a sign of Jane, but I shook my head
'*Look, Reach, Pull . . . 1,000, 2,000, 3,000, 4,000. . . .*

The canopy hesitated for a second and then burpe
into a quivering red jelly. After the whirlwind speed o
the descent, it was all too easy to stop concentratin
under canopy. And gradually, over the last few jumps
I'd started to look on the next five minutes of canop
control as just a formality.

I was flying downwind, admiring bits of Kent and
small aircraft taking off like a white insect, 1,500 fee
below me. So it wasn't until almost a minute ha
passed that I realised that, with the combined forwar
speed of the canopy and a ten mile an hour tailwind,
was scooting over the hedges at around 35 mph. A
ground level, though, there wasn't a flutter on eithe
of the windsocks, so I wasn't sure which way to land
In the end, I got it just about as wrong as I possibl
could. Both feet hit the ground with a sickenin
thump and I skidded forwards, coming to a stop 15 o
20 feet from where my heels had left their first mark i
the daisies.

From outside the Manifest Hut – at Drop Zon
Control – Paul Austin had been watching me fron
through the telemeter. Before I'd even reached th
packing sheds, he'd loped out towards me and put
hand on my shoulder.

'Miles, mate,' he said, 'a word in your shell-like
That landing was straight downwind and that isn'
good for your health.

Opposite
Paul Austin with an eye on the sky

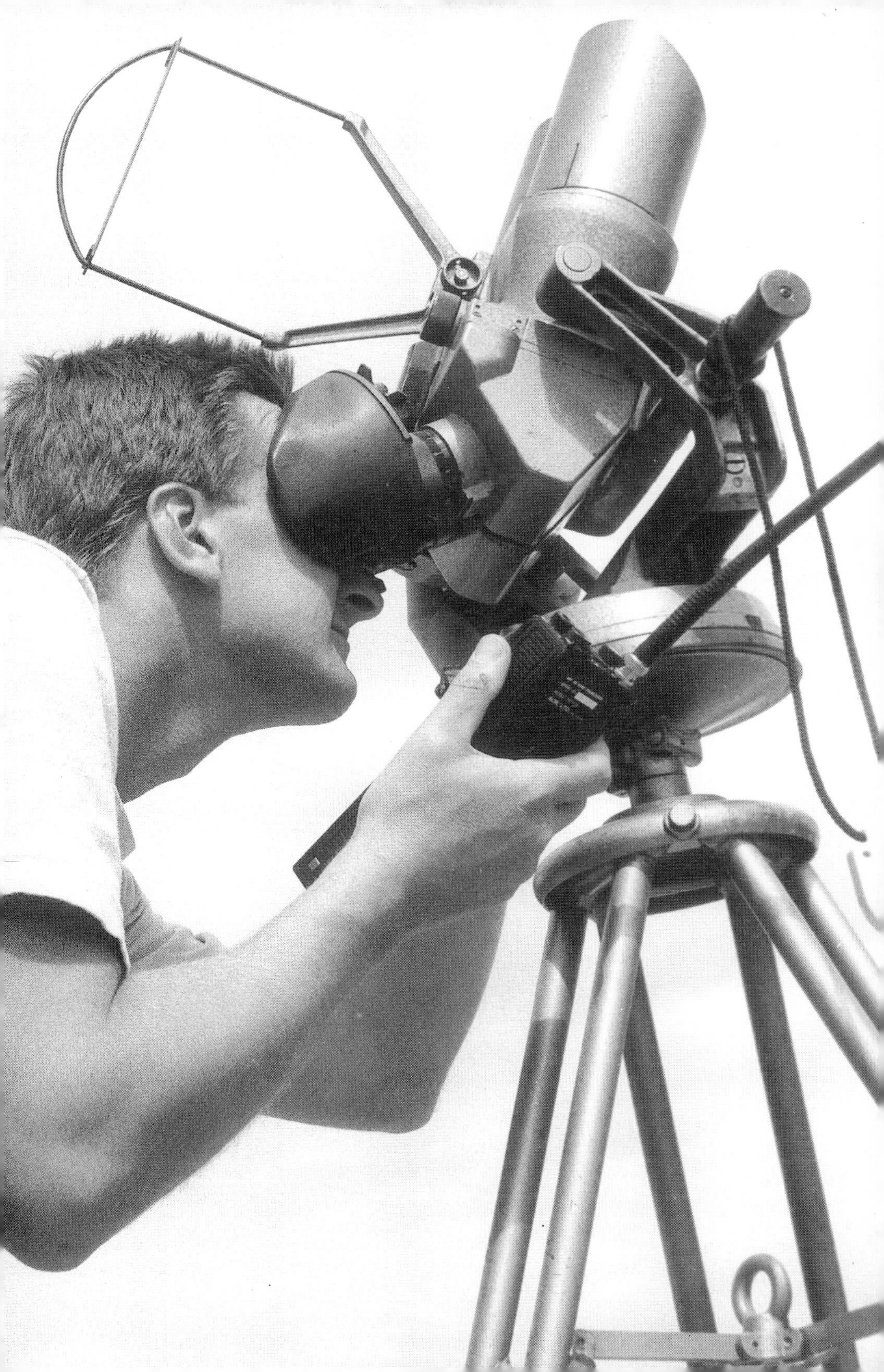

'I was watching you,' he said, 'and you had a change of heart at about 100 ft and started steering again. That's the *worst* possible thing you can do; you only just got your flare in in time. You *must* make your decision at 200 ft at the latest and then stick to it.'

I had my debrief as Jane was packing her rig. 'Okay, the exit was fine. I came out right behind you, and when I got down to you, I touched you on the arm and you looked across to me. Do you remember me doing that?'

It had only happened seven minutes ago, but I couldn't.

'Well, it was really just to tell you where I was. I gave you the thumbs up, and the first backloop was fine, except that you didn't arch out of it. You came back into the face-to-earth position and then you arched. On the second one, you wobbled a bit and turned left out of it, but no problem. You checked your alti and turned right for the track, and that was fine. But you said it yourself – your legs weren't straight. You went down and away from me and I was legging it along behind you. You leant off to the left and changed your heading which was good, but you could, in fact, have held the track for longer. Really there was nothing wrong with it – and I was right behind you when you shook your head.'

By the time I went in for the pull, she was right in front of me; if I'd only bothered to look up, I'd have seen her. Jane said, 'I was thinking, "Alright, you don't need me any more but you might at least look at me!" But anyway, I saw you wave off. And then you went into your old "*Woooop.* Legs up, back-slide routine" just before the pull.'

Nevertheless, I was *Cleared to Level VII*

It was already mid-day, and Level VII – the final dive before my Graduation Jump – was simply a question of putting into practice everything that I'd learnt. The only major difference was that it began with a Dive Exit.

I was back in the harness in the leaping frog position.

'Now, as soon as you've picked up a heading,' said Jane, 'I don't want you to wait for me. Just check your alti, and if you're at 9,000, your track can be for 10 seconds. If we're at 5,000 ft, obviously it'll have to be much shorter. I just want you to make maximum use of the time.

Level 7

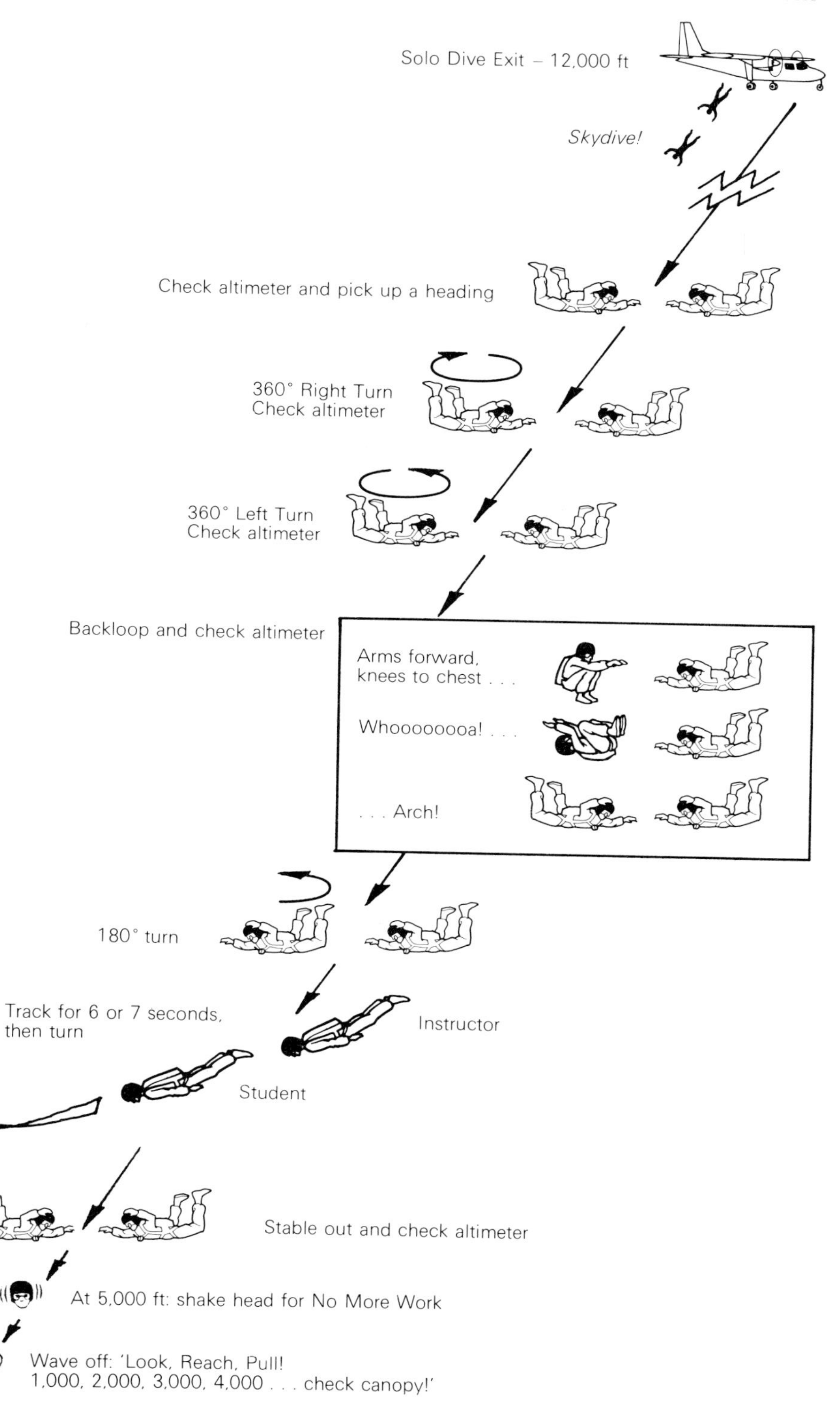
Solo Dive Exit – 12,000 ft
Skydive!
Check altimeter and pick up a heading
360° Right Turn
Check altimeter
360° Left Turn
Check altimeter
Backloop and check altimeter
Arms forward, knees to chest . . .
Whooooooooa! . . .
. . . Arch!
180° turn
Track for 6 or 7 seconds, then turn
Instructor
Student
Stable out and check altimeter
At 5,000 ft: shake head for No More Work
Wave off: 'Look, Reach, Pull!
1,000, 2,000, 3,000, 4,000 . . . check canopy!'

The Dive Exit: cruelty to the brain

'Do you understand what I mean by the relative wind?'

I didn't.

'Well, the easiest way to think of it, is as a slide at a 45 degree angle going down and away from the aircraft door, created by gravity and the forward movement of the aircraft. Now it doesn't really matter whether you go down the slide feet first or head first. A Dive Exit is exactly the reverse of what you do for a seated or 'stable' exit. In the first case you're head up, feet down; in the second your feet up, head down.'

That, Jane assured me, is the only difference. 'People will go through the door in all sorts of ways, but they'll generally present themselves to the slipstream in the proper way. To present equal areas of upper and lower body to the slipstream on a dive exit, your lower legs have to be dropped back and your arms pushed further forward. You "slide" down the slipstream in that position until you're in clear air.

then just flare into your normal stable position. The worst thing that can happen to you is that you'll go unstable – then all you do is arch. Basically, it's just a case of diving through the door.'

'Fine. Anything else?'

'Yes,' she said. 'This time, I want you to spot for the jump yourself.' The door would be opened for the run in; I'd have to shove my head out into the blast and watch the ground below, judging the moment that we were exactly the right distance upwind of the DZ.

Exactly 50 minutes after skidding to an undignified stop at the end of Level VII, I was back in the aircraft, climbing to altitude. It was the spotting that made me nervous. Mainly because there didn't seem to be an

Judging the exit
By noting the direction and distance that a Wind Drift Indicator (a tissue paper streamer dropped from 2,000ft) is carried downwind of the Target Arrow, the Jumpmaster can determine the right moment to leave the aircraft in order to reach the optimum opening point.

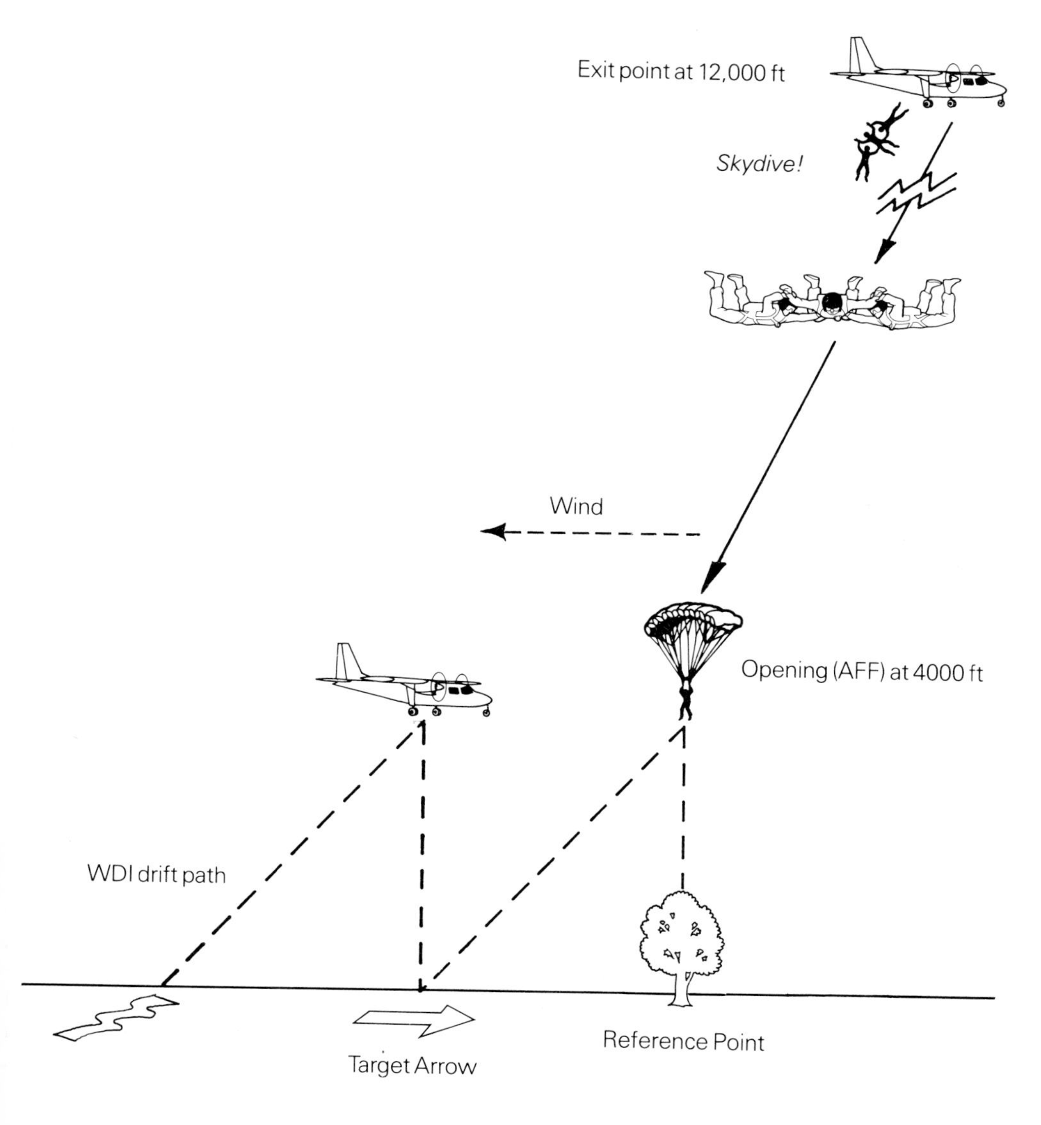

'You've got to imagine your way into each dive', said Rod. 'Try to create a series of pictures of the dive in your mind, so when you do it for real, you'll suddenly think, " Déjà vu. this is easy, I've been here before".'

exact point at which I should leave the aircraft; rather a line, 200 metres or so long, along which I could have chosen to jump at any moment. Until now, I'd studiously avoided the principle of Look Before You Leap, but now there wasn't much choice.

Even though the aircraft was still covering the ground at around 70 mph, from 12,000 ft the changes in the shape of the ground are slower and distant.

In no time, the aircraft had levelled out two and a half miles above the Slipsteam office. If I'd dropped a stone at that point, it would have landed on the canteen roof a minute and a half later.

Now the railway line was directly below us. I nodded at Jane and she pressed the middle button beside the door. The pilot throttled back the engines. I knelt by the opening for a second, and before I had time to think too hard about it, I simply rolled forward into the void. My weight and gravity took over, and I was plummeting towards the earth in the definitive headlong dive.

For perhaps three or four seconds, I was pointing vertically downwards, doing a sort of high altitude handstand but with open palms, and lower legs flopped down. For another two seconds, I thought I was going to roll on over onto my back. But forcing my arms out, I just swooped forward off the ramp of the slipstream.

I came stable very abruptly, rocking gently and then went, unbidden, into a right hand spin. When I'd regained control and stopped it, I just went through the exercises as though I was running through a shopping list.

Check alti, round to the right; check alti, round to the left; check alti, masses of height; a quick backloop, 180 degree right turn, lined up on a farm and then head down into the track.

Again, I held it straight for the first two or three seconds and then the buffeting started. I straightened out, buffeted again and eventually came stable for the pull. It was still only 4,000 ft, so I had time to look up at Jane who was grinning broadly. When the pull came, it was a little late at 3,300 ft.

Five minutes later, I landed gently beside the arrow. I didn't know it at the time, but this was to be my last debrief from Jane.

'Okay,' she said, 'the dive exit was really nice but then you started faffing about; I thought you were trying to go into your first turn. And surprise, surprise, you were back into your old, knees-down-bum-up position; you were just rushing. It looked as though you were fighting for stability and I was thinking, "Miles, if you just put your knees up" . . . and suddenly you did and you were fine.'

From there on everything had gone well – until it came to the pull. 'You were sitting up a bit and your pull was a good bit lower than 3,300. I pulled about two or three seconds after you and my canopy was open at 1,800 ft. I reckon you pulled at about 2,500 ft.'

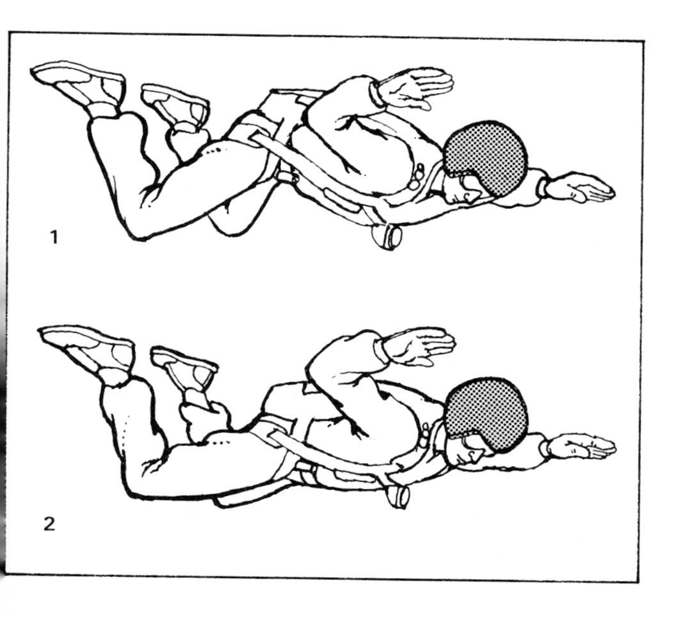

1 A bad bum-up-knees-down position, which will quickly result in buffeting, possibly even an airborne capsize and 2, a better arch.

'*Two* thousand, five hundred?'

She nodded. 'And to tell you the truth,' she admitted, 'I wasn't actually looking at my alti. It was probably a bit silly of me; because your altitude awareness has been so good, I wasn't worrying about it. I was waiting for you to pull.'

That, from one of Britain's leading freefall instructors, is honesty indeed. 'I still learn from things like that when they happen. In this case it's "Don't rely on a student even if they have shown very good altitude awareness all the way through."'

I knew why I'd done it. It was the first time I'd gone back to Free Time again; and I hadn't kept my eyes on the altimeter. But that, unbelievably, was Level VII.

Cleared to Level VIII.

'Right,' said Jane, 'get our names back on the board outside the Manifest Hut.'

'Done.'

'Good. Now, I'm going up with Colin this time. So Paul will watch your low level exit.'

At first, I felt abandoned and disappointed. 'But what about . . .' And then it occurred to me that since she wouldn't be leaving the aircraft with me anyway, I might as well get used to the idea of going it alone.

'What you've got to do is go up to just 4,500, get out of the aircraft, delay for about ten seconds and then pull. It's as simple as that. It's purely to show us that you can get stable within a short time of leaving the aircraft. It'll be a conventional seated exit; you go out facing into the slipstream as normal and try to keep on the same heading as the aircraft. The pull comes five to ten seconds after leaving the plane.

'The quicker you can pull the better because it's a short delay exercise. I don't want you to be unstable on the pull. And if for any reason, you're having problems getting stable then obviously, you must pull. Pull Height on this one is still 3,500.'

It was five past two. I had exactly one hour to do one jump. The skies parted like stage curtains and my name was called, among a list of people I hadn't met or jumped with. There was no Jane, no Jack or Steve.

The plane lifted off and I closed my eyes. 'Arch, stable, and pull.'

Someone left the plane at 3,500 ft and it was only then that the real implication of what I was about to do, hit me like a cold wave; a realisation that static line students have to come to terms with much earlier

Level 8 (Graduation Jump)

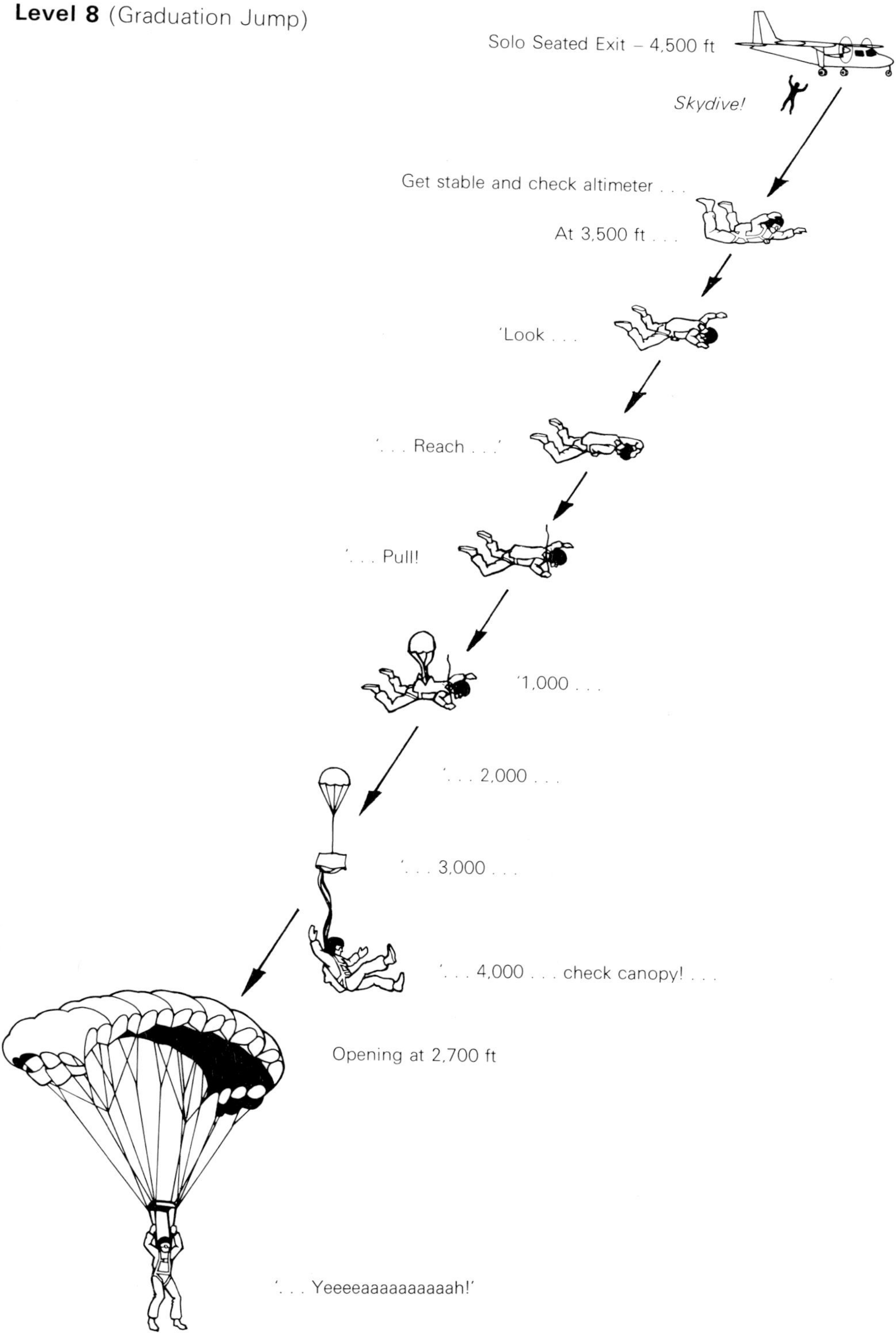

Solo Seated Exit – 4,500 ft

Skydive!

Get stable and check altimeter . . .

At 3,500 ft . . .

'Look . . .

'. . . Reach . . .'

'. . . Pull!

'1,000 . . .

'. . . 2,000 . . .

'. . . 3,000 . . .

'. . . 4,000 . . . check canopy! . . .

Opening at 2,700 ft

'. . . Yeeeeaaaaaaaaaah!'

in the training. It didn't matter that there was only ten seconds to get stable; I'd proved I could do that to Jane and myself. What did matter was that there would be no human life insurance policy flying beside me ready to grab the crucial handle if for some reason I decided not to bother.

Students on the conventional course get nervous as they progress to higher and higher jump altitudes at each stage of their training; but here was I, an AFF student, nervous about going down to a third of the normal jump altitude.

It had taken just five minutes for the aircraft to climb to 4,000 ft but for the last 500 ft, the hand crawled agonisingly round the dial. Paul Austin opened the door.

'Okay, mate. When you're ready.'

I sat in the doorway, and for the first time I felt very exposed and vulnerable, like a climber going solo on a well-known piece of rock. I felt precariously balanced; an extraordinary blend of fear and exhilaration. Yet I was relishing the fact that I was in complete control of a recognisable and very carefully calculated risk.

I pushed off, gasped, kicked at thin air, spun through 180 degrees, stabled out, saw the ground, waved my hands over my head, looked down at the main handle, reached for it, pulled it, counted to 4,000 and yelled my head off.

Three jumps in three and a half hours. More than enough to make up for hours of waiting around between jumps during the week. The average student takes ten to twelve jumps to achieve their Category 8. What AFF had taught me in ten jumps, Jane had had to learn in 64.

When you're qualified, risk becomes a line which you set for yourself. As one student pointed out, 'No one would ever just carry on jumping out and doing back loops or falling by themselves. You get to the stage where you say, "Right. I've done that. What's next?" Every time you jump, you achieve one more thing, and providing you keep those within the bounds of what is safe, you'll continue to enjoy the sport.'

Chris Francis, Headcorn's Chief Instructor, had a warning, 'There's a stage when an AFF student is, not necessarily in danger, but needs damping down slightly. Generally once he's completed his AFF course and he's around the 30 descent mark, he's beginning to reach the 'I've arrived" period. Well, I've done 3,000 parachute descents and I'm still waiting to arrive. That's something you've got to instil in everyone.'

Thirty-six hours later, Steve made his Graduation Jump and within a week he'd arranged to buy a rig of his own. Two days into the course, I'd asked him why he thought it was that he – rather than any of his friends – had ended up meeting this particular challenge.

'I'm not sure,' he said. 'I'm really a born coward, but I'm stubborn, you know: once I've set my mind on something, I'll finish it. The thing is,' he added, 'you can't think, "Perhaps I'll skydive." You must *want* to do it – and the only thing that requires a little courage is trying it once to see if you do.'

And his friends?

'Well, the funny thing is that they're all tempted by the idea. The temptation's there, but the courage to find out more about it isn't. They'd have to be dragged along to see how safe it is, and then they'd understand it.'

As Pete Gannaw had said: 'There'll always be doers and watchers. And most skydivers are what might be called "Edge-seekers". By that I mean that there are some people who seek definition to their world by finding the edges of it; and other people sit in the middle and look at the rest of it from the deep inside.'

It's still the sport with the dare-devil image. 'That will never go away completely. But, you know,' he told me one afternoon, pointing to the gateway into the airfield, 'the dare-devil part stops right about there, right when you step across the Whuffo Line.'

The magic certainly doesn't wear off. And very often, many miles from the nearest drop zone, I find myself looking for holes in the sky, and wondering whether or not I wouldn't rather be up among the clouds.

APPENDIX

Further reading

The Complete Sport Parachuting Guide Charles Shea-Simonds (A. & C. Black, London 1986)

Skydiving (Picture Library) Norman Barrett (Franklin Watts 1987)

Filming the Impossible Leo Dickinson (Jonathan Cape, 1982)

British AFF Centres

British Parachute School
The Control Tower
Langar Airfield
Langar
Nottingham
Tel: (0949) 60878

Flying Tigers Skydiving Centre
Goodwood Airfield
Near Chichester
West Sussex
Tel: (0243) 780333

Halfpenny Green Skydiving Centre
The Airfield
Bobbington
Near Stourbridge
West Midlands
Tel: (038 488) 293

London Skydiving Centre
Cranfield Airport
Cranfield
Bedford MK43 0AP
Tel: (0234) 751866

Slipstream Adventures
The Airfield
Headcorn
Kent TN27 9HX
Tel: (0622) 890641

Swansea Parachute Centre
Swansea Airport
Fairwood Common
Swansea
West Glamorgan
Tel: (0792) 296464

Thruxton Parachute Centre
Thruxton Airfield
Andover
Hampshire SP11 8PW
Tel: (0264) 772124

GLOSSARY

ACCELERATED FREEFALL (AFF) a rapid progression course in skydiving, which allows a student to freefall for 55 seconds from 12,000 ft (under instruction) just 6 hours after arriving at the airfield. A perfect AFF student can qualify to skydive unsupervised after just 8 jumps.

AUTOMATIC ACTUATION DEVICE(AAD) a safety device fitted on AFF rigs (*q.v.*), and operated by barometric pressure, which will deploy a student's reserve canopy at a predetermined height.

CANOPY RELATIVE WORK (CRW) the skill in which skydivers link up with open parachutes.

CIRCLE OF AWARENESS an exercise in becoming 'air-aware' – looking at the ground, reading the altimeter and reporting to the instructors.

CUT-AWAY DRILLS the endlessly rehearsed procedures for 'cutting away' or releasing yourself from a malfunctioning main canopy, and deploying the reserve.

DROP ZONE (DZ) a licensed skydiving area, normally surrounding an airfield.

FLARING almost stalling the parachute at the instant of touchdown to create the softest landing possible.

FREEFALL (OR SKYDIVING) the precious seconds of human flight *before* a parachute is deployed.

GROUND RUSH The sensation that the ground is rushing towards you on landing.

GROUND SPEED the speed at which a parachutist is moving over the ground (often less or more than air speed)

HOTEL CHECK an AFF's student's final words in the aircraft door.

PLF: PARACHUTE LANDING FALL the correct method of coming down to earth.

PILOT CHUTE a small parachute which deploys first in order to draw the larger (main or reserve) canopy smoothly out of its container.

PINNING docking with another skydiver in freefall

RAM AIR CANOPY the modern square canopy (used for main and/or reserve canopy), so called because air is rammed into its cells as the parachute glides forwards and down.

RIG the harness, parachutes and deployment devices worn by a skydiver.

RELATIVE WORK the skills of creating human freefalling formations. The record (in August 1988) was a formation of 144 skydivers, over Quincy, Illinois.

SPORT PARACHUTING the proper name for jumping out of planes

SLIPSTREAM the current of air created by the forward movement of the aircraft.

SQUAWK a numbered signal, issued daily to all aircraft, which provides Air Traffic Control with a continuous update on each aircraft's position and altitude.

STABLE POSITION the standard freefalling position, face-to-earth, with the arms and legs spread open to present a symmetrical surface to the airflow.

STACKING linking open parachutes (and parachutists), one above the other. The record in 1988 was 24.

STATIC LINE COURSE the slower conventional introduction to skydiving. For the first few jumps a student's parachute is opened automatically by a 'static line' fixed to the fuselage.

TANDEM JUMPING student jumping in dual harness with instructor

TELEMETER the skydiver's telescope, used for watching student's canopy control and in competition jumping.

TRACKING falling down and *across* the sky as a human missile.

WHUFFO anyone who doesn't jump out of aeroplanes

WIND SPEED the speed at which the air is moving over the ground.

Acknowledgements

I'm hugely grateful to the instructors of Slipstream Adventures at Headcorn, Britain's most active AFF centre, who introduced me to the thrills and skills of the sky. In particular, I must thank Chris Francis, (then Chief Instructor of the Headcorn Parachute Club), and two of Slipstream's owners – Pete and Debbie Allum – who immediately saw the value of a book on Accelerated Freefall. Rod Bartholomew, The Skydiving Moustache, was always encouraging, never alarmist. But above all, I was fortunate to spend my first five minutes in freefall in the company of Jane Buckle, four times British Ladies' Skydiving Champion, whose enormous experience, infectious enthusiasm and wacky sense of humour resulted in my successful qualifying jump on the eighth day.

My thanks, again, to Ian Dickens of Olympus Optical (UK) Ltd who provided the ever-reliable Olympus cameras and lenses which Simon Ward used for pictures in this book. For the air-to-air shots, two motor-driven *OM4Tis* were mounted on Simon's helmet with a purpose-made shutter release cable between his teeth.

As my fellow-AFF-student on this course, Stephen Saberi was wonderfully honest about his reactions to failure and later his success during the week. And if after reading this book, potential AFF students have a better idea of what they're letting themselves in for, they will owe much of that reassurance to his remarks.

Lastly, a special word of appreciation for the irrepressible Beverley B, who runs the office at Headcorn.